ALSO BY BRUCE PANDOLFINI:

Chess Target Practice
Pandolfini's Chess Complete
Beginning Chess
Chessercizes
More Chessercizes: Checkmate!
Chess Openings: Traps and Zaps
More Chess Openings: Traps and Zaps 2
Bobby Fischer's Outrageous Chess Moves
Square One
Principles of the New Chess
Pandolfini's Endgame Course
The ABC's of Chess
One-Move Chess by the Champions
Weapons of Chess
Russian Chess
Kasparov's Winning Chess Tactics

CHESS THINKING

BRUCE PANDOLFINI

A FIRESIDE BOOK
Published by Simon & Schuster
NEW YORK   LONDON   TORONTO   SYDNEY   TOKYO   SINGAPORE

FIRESIDE
Rockefeller Center
1230 Avenue of the Americas
New York, New York 10020

Copyright © 1995 by Bruce Pandolfini

FIRESIDE and colophon are registered trademarks
of Simon & Schuster Inc.

Designed by Stanley S. Drate/Folio Graphics Co. Inc.

Manufactured in the United States of America

10 9 8 7 6 5 4 3 2 1

Library of Congress Cataloging-in-Publication Data

Pandolfini, Bruce.
    Chess thinking / Bruce Pandolfini.
        p. cm.
    "A Fireside book."
    1. Chess—Dictionaries. I. Title.
GV1314.5.P36 1995
794.1'03—dc20   94-36737
                                              CIP

ISBN: 0-671-79502-3

For
Harry Fajans
and
Raymond Weinstein

ACKNOWLEDGMENTS

■

My thanks to Larry Tamarkin for producing the diagrams with Chess Base, and to Judy Shipman and International Master Walter Shipman for their research and insights on the openings index.

I would also like to thank Bruce Alberston, Carol Ann Caronia, Deirdre Hare, Rob Henderson, Burt Hochberg, and Idelle Pandolfini for their invaluable contributions to the manuscript, and my editor Kara Leverte for overseeing the entire project.

CONTENTS

■

Introduction

INTRODUCTION

■

Chess Thinking is not an encyclopedia. You won't find in it biographies of Alekhine, Botvinnik, or Capablanca. Nor is *Chess Thinking* a problem book, but somehow more than a hundred problems have slipped in. It's not even a book purely of instruction, though certainly my intent is to show and teach.

I prefer to think of it as more of a dictionary. Concepts are arranged alphabetically for ease of use, with abundant cross-references. Terms are defined and compared to other pertinent words. But like a quiz book, some are diagrammed with posed questions, the answers to which are right underneath or on the very next page. Finally, there's plenty of explanation and advice, just like a book of instruction.

What kinds of entries are there? All the standard chess words I could think of, but also included are slang, chess variants, recurring expressions and phrases, and helpful maxims and principles. There's also a smattering of items about computers, game theory, education, and general thinking which, though not really chess terms, are used quite often by chess teachers, writers, and players.

Any chessplayer can tap into *Chess Thinking*. Whether you start at the beginning and read through, or run checks on particular words, I believe you'll find a wealth of information to enhance your enjoyment of the game. However you experience chess—playing, reading, or thinking—you can expect to encounter semantic roadblocks to understanding. I offer *Chess Thinking* as a tool to clear the way.

ALGEBRAIC NOTATION

■

You can get more from this book if you understand algebraic notation, which is a way to record moves using letters and numbers. To start with, view the chessboard as an eight-by-eight grid. Every square on the grid has its own name, derived from the connecting files and ranks. Files, the lines of squares going up and down, are lettered a through h. Ranks, the lines of squares going across, are numbered 1 through 8. Squares are designated by combining letters and numbers; the letter is lowercase and appears first. Thus, in the starting position, White's queen occupies d1 and Black's queen occupies d8. All squares in the algebraic system are named from White's side. The algebraic grid given below indicates the names of all the squares. You might find it helpful to photocopy the grid and use it as a bookmark, so it's always there for review.

The algebraic grid. Every square has a unique name.

a8	b8	c8	d8	e8	f8	g8	h8
a7	b7	c7	d7	e7	f7	g7	h7
a6	b6	c6	d6	e6	f6	g6	h6
a5	b5	c5	d5	e5	f5	g5	h5
a4	b4	c4	d4	e4	f4	g4	h4
a3	b3	c3	d3	e3	f3	g3	h3
a2	b2	c2	d2	e2	f2	g2	h2
a1	b1	c1	d1	e1	f1	g1	h1

OTHER SYMBOLS

■

You will find it useful to learn the following symbols:

SYMBOL	MEANING
K	king
Q	queen
R	rook
B	bishop
N	knight
—	moves to
x	captures
+	check
+ +	checkmate
O-O	castles kingside
O-O-O	castles queenside

Note that pawns are not identified by a symbol. If no indication of the moving unit is given, it must be a pawn.

A

Absolute Pin A pin of a unit to its king. In this situation the pinned unit cannot legally move. See PIN and RELATIVE PIN.

Absolute Seventh Rank   See SEVENTH RANK ABSOLUTE.

Accumulation of Advantages   The strategy of building a position by gradually accumulating advantages, especially small or intangible ones.

The concept was originally stated by Wilhelm Steinitz (1836–1900), the first world champion. He argued that, though none of these "slight" pluses are necessarily important in themselves, their combined weight could lead to a winning position. They might not seem like much individually, but having just a little better mobility, space, king safety, flexibility, dynamism, and pawn structure often translates into a tremendous overall superiority. See POSITION PLAY.

Activate To develop, improve the position of, mobilize, or make more aggressive.

W: Ke2 Ra1 Ps a2 b2 d4 e3 f2 g2 h2 (9)

B: Kg8 Ra8 Ps a7 b7 d5 e6 f7 g7 h7 (9)

QUESTION: What is White's best move?

Pieces can be activated by transferring them to better squares or by moving something, usually a pawn, out of their way. Knights, bishops, and queens are mainly activated by moving them off the home rank toward the opponent. Rooks, on the other hand, become effective along the home rank when shifted to open or half-open files in order to attack the enemy position.

ANSWER: White gets the upper hand by activating the rook on a1 to the open file, 1. Rc1.

Active   Aggressive, as in active move, piece, variation, defense, or placement.

W: Kg2 Rf1 Bb3 Ps a2 b2 e2 f2 g3   (8)
B: Ke8 Ra8 Bh5 Ps a6 b7 c7 e6 f7   (8)

QUESTION: How should White defend the e-pawn?

An active piece is one that attacks. It asserts itself, as opposed to a passive piece, which merely defends or marks time. Similarly, an active defense deals with an enemy threat by combining protection with counterattack or by presenting a more immediate, serious, or relevant threat.

ANSWER: Black's bishop menaces White's e-pawn, which can be saved in a number of ways. The most active is not to guard the e-pawn but to hit back with 1. Rh1!. The bishop is then lost, for if it captures on e2 or moves to safety, White's rook checks on h8, skewering Black's king and rook.

Active Defense   One that combines defense with counterattack.

Active Rook   A rook positioned to attack, as opposed to a PASSIVE ROOK that is tied to defense; one that has the CHECKING DISTANCE.

Actual Play The real moves of a game, in contrast to possible variations.

Adjourn To break off a game intending to continue it later.

Adjourned Position The position on the board before a move is sealed. See ADJOURNMENT.

Adjournment A suspension of play until a later time.

In most tournaments and matches, a game may be adjourned after a specified number of moves and a certain amount of time has elapsed. The player to move writes down his next move and seals it in an envelope, which is not opened until the resumption of play. The sealing and subsequent opening of the envelope must be done in accordance with the official rules of chess. To find out more about the official rules, contact the U. S. Chess Federation, 186 Route 9W, New Windsor, N.Y., 12550 (or call 914-562-8350).

Adjudicate To decide the result of a game when circumstances prevent it from being concluded by actual play. This is done either by the tournament director or player designated by him.

Adjudication The act of deciding the result of a game without playing it out to a conclusion.

Adjust To center a piece or pawn precisely on its square. Before doing so one says "I adjust," "j'adoube," or something else clearly meaning the same thing. See TOUCH-MOVE.

Advance To move toward the enemy with a single piece or pawn or with several units in a general assault in a definite area of the board, as in "queenside advance," meaning queenside attack.

Advanced Pawn   One that has reached its fifth rank or farther, and thus has crossed the frontier line into enemy territory.

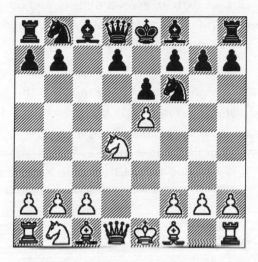

W: Ke1 Qd1 Ra1 Rh1 Bc1 Bf1 Nb1 Nd4 Ps a2 b2 c2 e5 f2 g2 h2   (15)

B: Ke8 Qd8 Ra8 Rh8 Bc8 Bf8 Nb8 Nf6 Ps a7 b7 d7 e6 f7 g7 h7   (15)

QUESTION: How should Black save the attacked knight?

An advanced pawn confers a spatial advantage along the file it occupies. For example, if there is a Black pawn on c3, White typically has access to the two squares in front of it (c1 and c2), while being able to assail a third (c3). Black meanwhile could utilize the five squares behind the pawn (c4, c5, c6, c7, and c8), eventually capitalizing on this c-file mobility edge. An advanced pawn is disadvantageous, however, when it's been pushed too far or without sufficient preparation. In such cases, the pawn, closer to the enemy and further from its lines of support, is overextended and prone to assailing forces and exploiting tactics. See OVEREXTENSION.

ANSWER: In the diagram, reached after the moves 1. e4 c5 2. Nf3 e6 3. d4 cxd4 4. Nxd4 Nf6 5. e5, Black doesn't have to move the endangered knight to save it. Instead Black can eliminate the attacking unit. White's prematurely advanced e-pawn is victimized by a fork, 5. . . . Qa5 +, followed by 6. . . . Qxe5 + .

Advantage Any kind of superiority, specific or overall.

The term especially applies, individually or in combination, to the elements of SPACE, TIME, MATERIAL, PAWN STRUCTURE, and KING SAFETY. By having the first move, White begins with a slight advantage in time, which he will try to convert into something more tangible.

Agreed Draw A prearranged draw in which the players follow a choreographed game or don't even bother to play. The practice is usually illegal and is always against the spirit of true competition.

An AGREED DRAW is not the same thing as a DRAW BY AGREEMENT. In the former, the players conspire before the game is played. In the latter, they decide to draw during the course of play.

Ahead In chess, having an advantage in material, position, or time.

Aimless Development Development for development's sake, not as part of an overall plan.

Algebraic Notation A method of recording chess moves in which the board is viewed as a coordinate grid.

A square in algebraic notation is designated by combining the letter of its file (a through h) with the number of its intersecting rank (1 through 8). A more complete explanation of the system, also known as *standard notation* or COORDINATE NOTATION, can be found on page 13. Curiously, the term algebraic notation is a misnomer, for it has nothing to do with algebra. See DESCRIPTIVE NOTATION.

Aligned Bishops Two friendly bishops on adjacent diagonals attacking in unison, often toward a particular sector, such as the kingside. See TWO-BISHOP SACRIFICE.

Allies Two or more players working as a team, either consulting on each move or playing moves alternately. If they have the white pieces they are the "white allies" and if the black pieces the "black allies."

Alternation Relying on a spatial edge to shift attacks between two different enemy weaknesses until the defender must make a concession. A term used by Aron Nimzovich (1886–1935), a great player and influential theorist.

Amateur A chessplayer who does not make a living from chess. Anyone who plays just for fun. See PROFESSIONAL.

Amaurosis Schacchistica Tarrasch's humorous expression for the "disease" of blundering repeatedly. Literally translated, it means "chess blindness." Siegbert Tarrasch (1862–1934), a great player early in this century, was a practicing physician. Also, the succession of white and black moves.

Ambush A term used in chess composition. It refers to a situation in which a piece moves behind a second piece, which when moving allows the first piece to come into play. Problemists call this a BATTERY if both pieces are the same color.

Analogue A comparable position or situation. A problem whose solution can be helpful in solving a related one.

Analysis The process of determining through careful examination the best moves in a variation or position.

The easiest situations to analyze are forced sequences, where the enemy has only one legal or reasonable move at each turn. In most positions your opponent has a number of decent responses, and if you try to look too far ahead your analysis becomes cumbersome, confused, time consuming, and even counterproductive. The trick is to start by making a mental list of CANDIDATE MOVES before analyzing any one move in depth. The art of it is deciding which moves are relevant enough to be included on this list.

Analyst   One who analyzes chess positions, particularly with proficiency. A THEORETICIAN.

Analytic Method   A technique for determining the best course of action by asking oneself pertinent questions. A method for planning.

Analyze   To investigate a position in detail to find the best continuations and to get at the truth.

Anastasia's Mate   A particular mating pattern relying on a rook and knight and typically requiring a setup queen sacrifice.

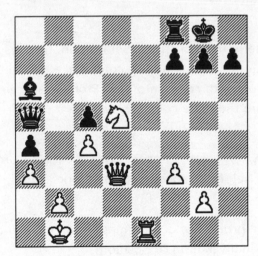

W: Kb1 Qd3 Re1 Nd5 Ps a3 b2 c4 f3 g2   (9)
B: Kg8 Qa5 Rf8 Ba6 Ps a4 c5 f7 g7 h7   (9)

QUESTION: Can White force mate?

The name is taken from the 1803 novel *Anastasia und das Schach-spiel,* by Wilhelm Heinse, but the mate referred to in the book (W: Kc7 Bb7 Pb6 B: Ka7) is not the one commonly signified as the pattern.

ANSWER: White can force Anastasia's Mate in three moves: 1. Ne7+

Kh8 2. Qxh7+ Kxh7 3. Rh1#. The knight is positioned to guard g8 and g6, the queen is sacrificed to open the h-file, and the rook gives the mating check—Anastasia's Mate.

Annihilation   A kind of undermining tactic whereby shielding defenses are destroyed or cleared away, usually by direct capture.

W: Kg1 Qg4 Rd1 Rg3 Ne4 Ps a2 c3 d4 f2 g2 h4   (11)
B: Kf7 Qd5 Rd8 Be7 Nf8 Ps a7 b7 c6 e6 g7 h6   (11)

QUESTION: How does White force mate?

Annihilation has another meaning in problem composition. There it refers to a theme by which a piece moving on a particular line is sacrificed so that another friendly piece may be able to use the same line. This is also called CLEARANCE.

ANSWER: In the diagram, White wins by denuding the Black king of necessary cover: 1. Qxg7+ Ke8 2. Qxe7+!! Kxe7 3. Rg7+ Ke8 4. Nf6#. By capturing the g7-pawn and the e7-bishop, White annihilates Black's control of f6, enabling White's knight to mate on that square.

Annotated Game A game with commentary. See ANNOTATION.

Annotation An explanation, clarification, note, aside, or simple comment on a move or variation.

Announced Mate A player's open declaration that mate can be forced in a specified number of moves. The practice is frowned upon in tournament play.

Answer The solution to a problem or the reply to a move or variation.

Ant A disparaging term for a player who memorizes opening moves but has no real understanding of them. Diverging from the book moves makes such a player feel lost. See FISH and FISHCAKE.

Anti-Positional Move A move that violates the spirit of a position by following the wrong strategy.

W: Kg1 Qd2 Re1 Be5 Ps e3 f2 g2 h3   (8)
B: Kg8 Qb7 Rf7 Nf5 Ps d5 e4 g7 h6   (8)

QUESTION: Should White play 1. g4 to drive away the knight?

Usually an anti-positional move is a pawn move made purely for immediate attack and without regard to longterm consequences. Anti-positional moves tend to produce chronic problems, for once a pawn moves past a square it can never protect it again.

ANSWER: The advance 1. g4, though it attacks the knight, is anti-positional because it permanently weakens f3, which can then be used by Black as a base of operations. The invasion 1. . . . . Nh4 soon gains at least the exchange.

Any   When used in the line score of a variation it means "any move," indicating that it is irrelevant.

In KRIEGSPIEL it's a typical question addressed to the referee, meaning "are there any legal captures?"

Arabian Mate   A mate given by a rook and knight in which the knight supports the rook while also guarding a potential escape square.

W: Kh1 Rg7 Nf6   (3)
B: Kh8 Ra2 Nf3   (3)

QUESTION: How many possibilities for Arabian Mate do you see?

The name undoubtedly comes from the occurrence of this mating pattern in certain 13th-century Arabic shatranj problems.

ANSWER: There are a total of three Arabian Mates. White can mate by either 1. Rg8# or 1. Rh7#; and, if it's Black's move, Black can give an Arabian Mate by 1. . . . Rh2#.

Arbiter   A tournament director or someone empowered to settle disputes and make decisions concerning an official event.

Arithmetic   Another word for CALCULATION.

Array   The starting setup at the beginning of a game. Also called the ORIGINAL POSITION.

Artificial Castling   See CASTLING BY HAND.

Associative Memory   A memory that stores data in parallel, so that one thought automatically triggers another.

Chessplayers tend to memorize this way, grouping information together in chunks so that one thing stands for many things. For example, if the situation is logically based, the placement of certain pawns should imply a relationship to the positioning of specific pieces with corresponding tactical possibilities.

Asymmetry   The term usually refers to an opening strategy (playing for asymmetry) in which one avoids a lifeless position, where both sides have similar deployments, by playing a move or following a plan that cannot be copied without disadvantage. It also denotes any general imbalance in a position that gives it character.

W: Kg1 Qd2 Ra1 Rf1 Bd3 Ps a2 c2 f2 g2 h2 (10)

B: Kg8 Qd7 Ra8 Rf8 Bd6 Ps a7 c7 f7 g7 h7 (10)

QUESTION: Should White break the symmetry by Bd3-e4?

Typical ways to disturb symmetry include checking, capturing, or merely threatening, but sometimes it's just a matter of playing a different move. In trying to maintain symmetry the second player must be particularly careful, for once mated he doesn't get last licks.

ANSWER: It's true that Black shouldn't follow suit and play 1. . . . Be5, for that would expose the queen to a free capture (2. Qxd7). But White's move (1. Be4) is a queen-losing blunder: 1. . . . Bxh2+! 2. Kxh2 Qxd2.

Attack A move or series of moves to mate, gain material, or obtain advantage. It also means to make or threaten such moves.

W: Ke1 Bf1 Nf3 Ps b2 c3 e4 f2   (7)
B: Ke7 Be5 Nc6 Ps b6 c7 e6 f7   (7)

QUESTION: Can White win material?

More narrowly, an attack is the mere placement of a unit in position to capture another, not necessarily with advantage. You "attack" when positioned to capture, but "threaten" only if the planned capture is desirable.

ANSWER: In the diagram, White's knight is attacking Black's bishop but doesn't threaten it because the bishop is satisfactorily defended for the moment. However, with 1. Bb5 White attacks the c6-knight and threatens to remove the e5-bishop's support. Even if Black guards c6 with his king, White exchanges bishop for knight (Bb5xc6), and then captures on e5 for free.

Attack at the Base of the Pawn Chain A maxim encapsulating a strategy first articulated by Aron Nimzovich.

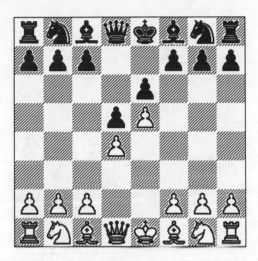

W: Ke1 Qd1 Ra1 Rh1 Bc1 Bf1 Nb1 Ng1 Ps a2 b2 c2 d4 e5 f2 g2   (16)
   h2

B: Ke8 Qd8 Ra8 Rh8 Bc8 Bf8 Nb8 Ng8 Ps a7 b7 c7 d5 e6 f7 g7   (16)
   h7

QUESTION: How should Black proceed?

When a chain of White pawns are held in place by a chain of Black ones, so that none of them can move, it's usually advisable to attack the enemy pawns at the base of their chain (the pawn closest to the opponent's home rank). The point is to undermine the chain by knocking out its foundation. For example, in the Advance Variation of the French Defense (1. e4 e6 2. d4 d5 3. e5), White's base is the pawn at d4, and Black's is the pawn at e6. The pawn at f7 is technically not part of the black chain because it can move (no white pawn blocks it).

ANSWER: Black should start the assault against the base of White's pawn chain by playing 3. . . . c5, with the idea of weakening White's support of e5. By the same token, White would like to push the pawn on f2 to f5, attacking Black's base; but this takes an extra move and is not immediately practical.

Attraction   Forcing a unit to a particular square in order to exploit it. Also called DRIVING ON.

W: Ke1 Nf4 Pg2   (3)
B: Kc8 Ne3 Ph4   (3)

QUESTION: Does Black have a winning tactic?

Attractions draw defending units to vulnerable points so that other tactical possibilities emerge. A common attraction theme is to force a square to be blocked, as a queen sacrifice does in a typical SMOTH-ERED MATE.

ANSWER: Black wins by 1. . . . Nxg2 + !, when 2. Nxg2 is murdered by 2. . . . h3, leading to a new queen.

B

B   The standard abbreviation for bishop.

Back Rank   The rank occupied by the eight enemy pieces in the starting position; a player's last rank. Less precisely, either the first or eighth rank. Also called BACK ROW.

Back-Rank Mate A CORRIDOR MATE given by a queen or rook along the enemy's home rank when the losing king is unable to escape because it's blocked or trapped. Also called a BACK-ROW MATE.

W: Kh5 Qh1   (2)
B: Kh8   (1)

QUESTION: How can White mate in two moves?

Chessplayers often misuse this term for any line-mate by a queen or rook along any edge of the board, whether rank or file. All queen and rook line-mates are corridor mates, but only those given along outside ranks are also back-rank mates.

ANSWER: In the diagram, White can force a back-rank mate in two moves by 1. Kg6+ Kg8 2. Qa8#.

Back Rook When friendly rooks are doubled on a line, the back rook is the second one, the one that supports the invasion of the forward rook. See FRONT ROOK.

Back Row Another name for BACK RANK.

Back-Row Mate Another name for BACK-RANK MATE.

Backward Pawn A pawn whose neighboring pawns are too far advanced to protect it.

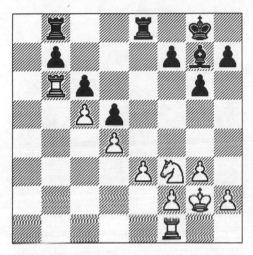

W: Kg2 Rb6 Rf1 Nf3 Ps c5 d4 e3 f2 g3 h2   (10)

B: Kg8 Rb8 Re8 Bg7 Ps b7 c6 d5 f7 g6 h7   (10)

QUESTION: Can White win a pawn?

A backward pawn is usually a weakness, especially if it is restrained by enemy pieces and pawns and is subject to frontal attack by major pieces along the file. The backward pawn's actual or practical inability to move renders it a target and tends to produce a defensive, cramped position with blocked lines and limited scope.

ANSWER: A backward pawn's inherent weakness may result in the vulnerability of nearby friendly pawns. In the diagram, Black has a backward b-pawn obstructed by a White rook. After 1. Rfb1, attacking b7 for a second time, Black must lose a pawn. The b-pawn's only defense 1. . . . Re7, is answered by 2. Rxc6, when 2. . . . bxc6 allows 3. Rxb8 + .

Bad Bishop A bishop whose mobility is reduced by blocked or fixed pawns on squares the same color as those used by the bishop.

W: Kg5 Ne4 Ps a5 b4 c5   (5)
B: Kg7 Bc8 Ps a6 b5 c6 d7   (6)

QUESTION: How can White exploit the bad bishop?

A bad bishop can be opposed by a good bishop or a good knight. In either case, the defender's remedy tends to be an exchange of minor pieces, though this is harder to effect when the pieces are un-alike (bishop vs. knight).

ANSWER: In the diagram, Black's bad bishop is obstructed by its own pawns. If the knight invades (1. Nd6), the bishop is lost.

Bad Check A check that wastes time or incurs disadvantage. See POINTLESS CHECK.

Knowing when to check is a fine art. As a rule, if you don't see that a check results in certain advantage, don't give it. Save it for a more pivotal time, when you need it or your opponent has forgotten about it.

Balance Equilibrium; a general equality, where one side's advantages are roughly offset by the opponent's.

Balance of Position The situation of having comparable advantages and weaknesses, so that neither side has a distinct edge. See EQUILIBRIUM.

Balanced Pawn Structure A position in which every white pawn is on the same file as a black pawn.

Bare King A king by itself, without any other same-color units on the board. Also called a LONE KING.

Barrier Usually a rank or file occupied and controlled by either a queen or rook, preventing the enemy king from escaping or participating. See CUTOFF.

W: Kg2 Ra1 Rd4 Ps a2 b3 g3 (6)
B: Kh8 Ra8 Re8 Ps a7 e6 f7 (6)

QUESTION: How should White snare the black king?

Actually, any line piece can establish a barrier, since queens and bishops can form them on diagonals. A particularly powerful barrier is a double one created by two friendly bishops occupying consecutive diagonals.

ANSWER: By playing 1. Rg4, White traps the black king on the h-file. Next move White mates by checking on h1.

Base of the Pawn Chain
In a fixed chain of interlocked black and white pawns, the base is the pawn, for each side, closest to its own home rank. See PAWN CHAIN and ATTACK AT THE BASE OF THE PAWN CHAIN.

W: Ke1 Ps d5 e4 f3 (4)
B: Ke8 Ps c7 d6 e5 (4)

QUESTION: Where is the base of the pawn chain?

A true pawn chain consists of linked black and white strands. There are two bases, one for White and one for Black.

ANSWER: In the diagram, White's base is at e4 and Black's at d6. Note that though the pawns at f3 and c7 are connected to other pawns, neither is considered part of the chain because they can move.

Basic Center The actual center of the board, consisting of the four squares d4, d5, e5, and e4.

Basic Mate Any of four elementary checkmates that can be forced against a lone king by four different combinations of pieces.

W: Kf7 Bg5 Ne7 (3)

B: Kh8 (1)

QUESTION: How can White mate in three moves?

The four standard basic mates are king and queen vs. king; king and rook vs. king; king and two bishops vs. king; and king, bishop, and knight vs. king.

ANSWER: In the diagram, White can force a typical bishop-and-knight basic mate in three moves: 1. Ng6+ Kh7 2. Nf8+ Kh8 3. Bf6#.

Basics Necessary information that every chessplayer should know, including the moves and rules, simple mates and tactics, essential endgames, and useful opening principles. Similar to FUNDAMENTALS.

Battery In problem composition, an AMBUSH in which both pieces are of the same color. In ordinary usage, two or more pieces of like power attacking supportively along the same line.

W: Kg1 Qb3 Re2 Ba2 Ng5 Ps f4 g3   (7)
B: Kh8 Qd6 Rf8 Bc7 Nd4 Ps g7 h7   (7)

QUESTION: How can White mate in two moves?

Two rooks or a queen and rook can form batteries along ranks and files, and a queen and bishop can be a battery on a diagonal.

ANSWER: White's queen-and-bishop battery forces mate: 1. Qg8+ Rxg8 2. Nf7#.

Bayonet Attack In any opening or variation, the sharp pawn thrust g2-g4 played to open the g-file, to seize control mainly of f5, and/or to threaten to dislodge the f6-knight, gaining control of d5 and e4. Also, the comparable advance for Black (g7-g5) with similar threats.

BB Abbreviation for black bishop.

Beauty Prize A prize sometimes awarded in tournaments for the most beautiful or brilliant game. See BRILLIANCY PRIZE.

Beginner Someone who is just beginning to learn about the game.

Although a beginner knows little about chess, it's not fair to describe a newcomer as weak. To be considered "weak" one must have studied or played seriously for years with no visible improvement.

Behind a Passed Pawn A phrase usually applied to rook endings, describing the most effective placement for a rook with regard to a passed pawn.

W: Ke3 Ra2 Ps b7 f2 g3 h4 (6)
B: Ke7 Rb8 Ps f7 g6 h5 (5)

QUESTION: How should White defend the b-pawn?

When a rook is stationed behind a passed pawn on the same file, the mobility of the rook increases as the pawn advances. This is true whether the rook is attacking an enemy pawn or supporting the advance of a friendly one. The opposite results when a rook is positioned in front of a pawn. The rook's mobility along the same file decreases as the pawn advances.

ANSWER: 1. Rb2! freezes Black's rook in place. If it moves, unless it can do so with check, White's b-pawn promotes with protection. So Black's fragile defense will hinge solely on the king—a severe disadvantage.

Best by Test A famous phrase used by Bobby Fischer in a 1964 *Chess Life* article to describe White's first-move choice 1. e4.

Biffing the Bishop Attacking an aggressively posted bishop that is attacking one's own knight, attempting to force it either to take the knight or retreat. See PUTTING THE QUESTION TO THE BISHOP.

Bind A situation in which one side's space is greatly reduced by the opponent's forces, especially restraining pawns, making it difficult to relieve the cramped situation by a liberating advance.

If you have your opponent in a bind, avoid freeing exchanges. Don't release the cramp until you can convert your spatial edge into something more concrete. If you are in a bind, seek to exchange pieces for breathing room, especially your most ineffective units. Make sure to do so, however, without precipitating other problems.

Bishop A minor piece, one of the six different types of chess units. Bishops move only on diagonals. Each side starts with two, a dark-square bishop and a light-square bishop. A bishop is about equal to a knight, which is worth about three pawns. The standard abbreviation for bishop is B.

Bishop Ending An ending characterized by bishops and pawns.

Bishop of the Wrong Color
Also called WRONG-COLOR BISHOP or WRONG BISHOP. A bishop that can't guard a friendly rook-pawn's promotion square. See FORTRESS and POSITIONAL DRAW.

W: Ka1 Bd1   (2)
B: Kc6 Bd5 Ps a3 b5   (4)

QUESTION: Can White salvage a draw?

A position in which one side has a bishop and two pawns (one of which is a rook-pawn whose promotion square can't be protected by its own bishop) and the other side has a lone minor piece may present an unusual opportunity for the weaker side. If circumstances allow, the player without the pawns might be able to sacrifice the minor piece for the opposing "good pawn," leaving the opponent with a rook-pawn whose promotion square can't be controlled. To draw, the defending king merely occupies the corner promotion square, and the attacker is unable to force it away without allowing stalemate.

ANSWER: In the diagram, White, though behind by two pawns, can force a draw by the pinning 1. Ba4!. However Black responds, his b-pawn disappears (or becomes an a-pawn by taking the bishop), and White draws by keeping the king in contact with a1, maintaining the fortress.

Bishop Pair The advantage of having two bishops against the opposition's bishop and knight or two knights. See TWO BISHOPS.

Bishop-Pawn A pawn on the c-file or the f-file.

Bishops of Opposite Colors Also called *opposite-color bishops*. A situation, particularly germane to the endgame, in which one player has a bishop moving on light squares and the other player has a bishop moving on dark squares.

W: Ke1 Ba7 (2)
B: Kc2 Bc4 Ps d3 e2 (4)

QUESTION: Can White stop the pawns?

Since bishops of opposite colors can never attack each other directly, endings including them often end in bloodless draws, with the defender setting up blockades on squares guarded by its bishop.

ANSWER: In the diagram, White can draw by 1. Be3, stopping the advance of the d-pawn. White holds by sustaining his double guard on d2, safely marking time with the bishop along the d2-h6 diagonal. Black's bishop can only watch idly, unable to check the white king.

Biting on Granite A way to characterize a bishop that lacks scope. A bishop on a diagonal that is blocked by enemy pawns is so frustrated that it might as well be attacking rock. Also used to describe a rook on a half-open file assailing an enemy pawn solidly protected by one or two other pawns.

BK The abbreviation for black king.

Black The player who goes second at the start of the game and who has the dark-colored pieces.

The dark-colored pieces are referred to as black regardless of their actual color. For instructional purposes it helps to distinguish between pieces and squares. Pieces are white and black, squares are light and dark.

Black-Square Bishop Another name for DARK-SQUARE BISHOP.

Black Squares Also called DARK SQUARES.

Black to Play and Win Also given as *Black to move and win.* A stipulation or caption indicating that Black plays a move that forces a winning situation. This is seen far less often than the conventional WHITE TO PLAY AND WIN or *White to move and win.*

Blindfold Chess Standard chess where at least one of the combatants plays without sight of the board.

A blindfold player either sits with his back to the board or is actually blindfolded. In either case the moves are conveyed by chess notation.

Blind Side The most vulnerable side in situations in which a defending unit must ward off invasions from either of two sides.

W: Kf5 Ps b6 e7 f6 (4)
B: Kd7 Ps b7 f7 (3)

QUESTION: How should White proceed?

In pawn endings, the stronger king usually tries to invade on the defender's blind side when such an option exists.

ANSWER: In the diagram, White wins by invading with the king on the blind side (here, toward the kingside), going from f5 to g5 to h6 to g7 (and even to g8 if White needs to gain a tempo).

Blindsided To be attacked where least expected or on the side most difficult to defend.

Blind Swine Mate   A mate given by a battery of two rooks along the seventh rank.

W: Kh1 Ra7 Rf7   (3)
B: Kh8 Ra8 Rf8   (3)

QUESTION: How can White mate in two moves?

Two rooks on the seventh rank are an awesome force even when they can't bring about immediate mate. The rooks support each other and the threat to mate is always there—one rook ready to shift to the last rank, the other retaining control of the seventh.

ANSWER: White has a blind swine mate by 1. Rh7+ Kg8 2. Rag7#.

Blitz   Speed chess. See RAPID TRANSIT CHESS.

Block   To OBSTRUCT a square or line. Also, the obstruction itself.

Blockade A strategy to prevent the advance of an enemy pawn, particularly a passed or isolated one, by positioning a piece, especially a knight, in front of the pawn and guarding that square with other pieces and pawns.

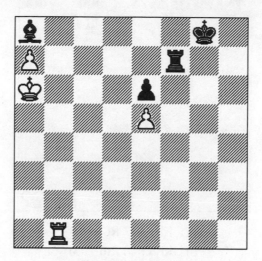

W: Ka6 Rb1 Ps a7 e5 (4)
B: Kg8 Rf7 Ba8 Pe6 (4)

QUESTION: How does White break the blockade?

An isolated pawn should be blockaded to prevent its advance and subsequent exchange for a healthy friendly pawn. A passed pawn should be blockaded to stop it from becoming a threat to queen.

ANSWER: Not all pieces blockade well. In the diagram, the bishop successfully blockades White's a-pawn. White wins by replacing the good blockader (the bishop) with a bad one (the rook): 1. Rb8+ Rf8 2. Rxa8!. A likely conclusion is 2. . . . Rxa8 3. Kb7 Rf8 4. a8/Q Rxa8 5. Kxa8 Kf7 6. Kb7 Kg6 7. Kc6 Kf5 8. Kd6. White wins Black's pawn and soon makes a new queen.

Blocked Obstructed; immobilized by pawns, without a clear path. A line is especially blocked if friendly pawns get in the way, because you can't go through your own pawns. To unclog such a line, look to exchange off the pawn impediments.

Blocked Center A situation in which interlocked white and black pawns prevent access or movement through the center.

Blocked Pawn A pawn that can't move because the square in front of it is occupied by an enemy unit.

Blunder A serious mistake or gross oversight that either loses or throws away a winning game.

BN The abbreviation for black knight.

Board Short for CHESSBOARD.

Boden's Mate A mate, typically set up by a queen sacrifice, given by the crisscross action of two bishops.

W: Kd2 Qf3 Be2 Bf4 Nc3 Ps b2 b4 c2 d4 f2 g2 h3 (12)
B: Kc8 Qh1 Rd8 Rh8 Nd7 Ng8 Ps a7 b7 c6 e6 f7 g7 h7 (13)

QUESTION: How can White force mate in two moves?

The name comes from Samuel Boden (1826-82) who in 1853 played an offhand game in London (Schulder–Boden) that went 1. e4 e5 2.

Nf3 d6 3. c3 f5 4. Bc4 Nf6 5. d4 fxe4 6. dxe5 exf3 7. exf6 Qxf6 8. gxf3 Nc6 9. f4 Bd7 10. Be3 O-O-O 11. Nd2 Re8 12. Qf3 Bf5 13. O-O-O d5 14. Bxd5 Qxc3+ 15. bxc3 Ba3#.

ANSWER: White mates by 1. Qxc6+ bxc6 2. Ba6#. The position is from the game Canal–Amateur, Budapest 1934.

Book Published theory, mainly of the opening and sometimes the endgame.

Book Draw A position that endgame books give as drawn.

Book Ending A position, usually a general case, that can be found in endgame texts with appropriate procedures and supportive variations.

Book Move In a specific opening variation, the recommended or most usual move given in the standard critical manuals.

Book Player One who relies more on published analysis than on original ideas. Generally, a predictable, unimaginative player who lets others do the thinking.

BP The abbreviation for black pawn. Also the abbreviation for bishop-pawn (one on the a-file or the f-file).

BQ The abbreviation for black queen.

BR The abbreviation for black rook.

Break A freeing move or maneuver, usually a pawn advance.

Breaking the Pin Inserting a friendly piece on the line of the pin so that the pin no longer has any force. Also, driving away the pinning piece.

Breakthrough Typically a pawn move (or moves) to clear lines for penetration into enemy territory, often by means of a sacrifice.

W: Kh1 Ps a5 b5 c5 (4)
B: Kh3 Ps a7 b7 c7 (4)

QUESTION: Can White sneak a pawn through to queen?

Some breakthroughs are targeted for aggression, to release attacking forces against the opposing king, but many are made to create a passed pawn that will go on to queen.

ANSWER: The diagram illustrates a common breakthrough combination. White starts by advancing the middle pawn, 1. b6. If 1. . . . axb6, then 2. c6 bxc6 3. a6 wins. Or if 1. . . . cxb6, then 2. a6 bxa6 3. c6 does the trick.

Breakthrough Combination See BREAKTHROUGH.

Brevity A short game, typically 20 moves or fewer, containing incisive tactics and usually showing how to exploit violations of principle.

W: Kc1 Qb3 Rd1 Bg5 Ps a2 b2 c2 e4 f2 g2 h2   (11)
B: Ke8 Qe6 Rh8 Bf8 Nd7 Ps a7 e5 f7 g7 h7   (10)

QUESTION: How did Paul Morphy mate in two moves?

Perhaps the most famous brevity of all time was a game played at the Paris Opéra in 1858 between Paul Morphy (White) and a team of two amateurs (Black), Count Isouard and the Duke of Brunswick. It began 1. e4 e5 2. Nf3 d6 3. d4 Bg4 4. dxe5 Bxf3 5. Qxf3 dxe5 6. Bc4 Nf6 7. Qb3 Qe7 8. Nc3 c6 9. Bg5 b5 10. Nxb5 cxb5 11. Bxb5+ Nbd7 12. O-O-O Rd8 13. Rxd7 Rxd7 14. Rd1 Qe6 15. Bxd7+ Nxd7 (see diagram).

ANSWER: Morphy won by sacrificing his queen to clear the d-file for his rook: 16. Qb8+ Nxb8 17. Rd8#.

Bridge A blocking move, usually by a rook, to stop enemy checks, usually from a rook. See LUCENA'S POSITION and BUILDING A BRIDGE.

Brilliancy A brilliant combination leading to a quick victory. Also, a short game containing ingenious tactics. Similar to BREVITY.

W: Kg1 Qf2 Ra1 Rd1 Ba3 Nc3 Nd4 Ps a2 b3 g3 h2   (11)
B: Kg8 Qh3 Ra8 Re8 Bb7 Bg7 Ps a7 b6 f7 g6 h7   (11)

QUESTION: How does Black force a win?

An example of a short game offering brilliant play is the contest between Robert Byrne (White) and Bobby Fischer (Black) played in the U.S. Championship, 1963-64. It started 1. d4 Nf6 2. c4 g6 3. g3 c6 4. Bg2 d5 5. cxd5 cxd5 6. Nc3 Bg7 7. e3 O-O 8. Nge2 Nc6 9. O-O b6 10. b3 Ba6 11. Ba3 Re8 12. Qd2 e5 13. dxe5 Nxe5 14. Rfd1 Nd3 15. Qc2 Nxf2 16. Kxf2 Ng4+ 17. Kg1 Nxe3 18. Qd2 Nxg2 19. Kxg2 d4 20. Nxd4 Bb7+ 21. Kf1 Qd7 and White resigned (0-1).

ANSWER: The diagram position would have been reached if the game had continued with the moves 22. Qf2 Qh3+ 23. Kg1. Fischer would have won by 23. . . . Re1+!! 24. Rxe1 Bxd4, when the pinned white queen is unable to thwart Black's mate at g2.

Brilliancy Prize An award sometimes given at the end of a tournament for the most ingenious attacking game.

Brute Force   A term describing the way some computer programs determine their moves: by sheer calculation of all possibilities. See PARALLEL ARCHITECTURE.

Bughouse   Team chess played on two or more boards in which captured pieces are given to teammates to be used on their own boards when needed. Each putback counts as a move. The first player to mate wins for his team. Also called DOUBLE BUGHOUSE and TANDEM PUTBACK.

Building a Bridge   In rook endings, a technique to create shelter for a king and/or passed pawn.

W: Kb8 Rd1 Pb7   (3)
B: Ke7 Ra2   (2)

QUESTION: How does White shield the king from checks?

In the diagram, White's king is unable to move from in front of the pawn without being harassed by rook checks. White solves this problem by deploying the rook so that it can eventually block the checks.

ANSWER: White first stations the rook on its fourth rank, 1. Rd4!. An illustrative variation from there is: 1. . . . Ra1 2. Kc7 Rc2+ 3. Kb6 Rb2+ 4. Kc6 Rc2+ 5. Kb5! Rb2+ 6. Rb4, and the pawn promotes.

Bust. A refuted opening line or tactic. Also, to show to be unsound or wrong.

Busted Position   A hopeless, resignable situation.

Bust Up   To ruin the enemy's pawn structure, particularly in front of the castled king, either by capture or sacrifice.

Busted Variation   A refuted line that should be abandoned.

Bye   In tournaments, advancing to the next round without playing because a pairing isn't possible or for some other practical reason approved by the director. Players receiving byes get either a full or half point depending on the rules of the event.

C

Caissa The muse or goddess of chess, from an 18th-century poem by Sir William Jones.

Calculation The process of analyzing and evaluating specific moves and variations, as opposed to making general judgments and assessments. Sometimes called ARITHMETIC.

Calculation of Variations See CALCULATION.

Camp A player's half of the board; later on, a player's main stronghold, especially around the king.

Candidate See CANDIDATE MOVE and CANDIDATE PASSED PAWN.

Candidate Move   A reasonable move, worthy of analysis or consideration. Also called CANDIDATE.

Before analyzing a situation in depth, whether during a game or
while solving a problem, start by forming a mental list of moves to be
considered—the candidate moves. Although the list might be superfi-
cial, it fulfills several functions. You can't analyze every move in a
position, so it makes sense to determine the most relevant ones before
proceeding. The forming of a list tends to reduce possibilities even
further, for some moves may be rejected on immediate comparison.
The list can be a reminder. If an initial selection gets nowhere, turn
back to the list for other candidates. During clock games the list lets
you apportion time better. The list can be a synthesizer, allowing several moves to be combined in an overall solution. Finally, forming any
kind of list imposes order, which can only be helpful.

Candidate Passed Pawn   In any group of pawns, the one likely
to become passed, that is, with no enemy pawn in front of it on the
same file. Also called CANDIDATE.

W: Kg1 Ps a2 b2 c2 g2 h2   (5)
B: Kg8 Ps a7 b7 c7 f7 g7 h6   (6)

QUESTION: Which pawn is the candidate?

The chief advantage of a candidate passed pawn is that it could be converted into an endgame weapon—a passed pawn, which could then be advanced. The pawn then might be promoted directly or, in its inexorable march, divert enemy forces from other chores.

ANSWER: Black's f-pawn is the candidate. With correct play it has a chance to emerge as a passed pawn.

Capablanca's Rule A rule of thumb, attributed to José Raúl Capablanca (1888–1942), that recommends mobilizing a pawn majority by first advancing the unopposed pawn—the one with no enemy pawn in front of it on the same file.

W: Ka1 Ps g3 h3   (3)
B: Kc1 Pg6   (2)

QUESTION: Which pawn should White advance first?

A typical way to create a passed pawn is by applying Capablanca's Rule. Once you have a passed pawn, try to shepherd it toward promotion in a timely yet prudent way. It either becomes a new queen or is used as a DECOY to score elsewhere on the board.

ANSWER: In the diagram, White wins by advancing the h-pawn first (1. h4), and then the other pawn (2. g4). Starting instead with the g-pawn (1. g4?) allows 1. . . . g5!, and both white pawns are held back.

Capture   The removal of an enemy unit. Also, to take an opposing piece or pawn.

Castle   To move the king and rook on the same turn. See CASTLING and LOST THE RIGHT TO CASTLE. Also, a common but unofficial name for the rook.

Castle by Hand   To achieve the effect of castling by moving the king and rook individually over the course of several moves, usually done after the king has LOST THE RIGHT TO CASTLE. Also called ARTIFICIAL CASTLING.

Castle Early   A maxim advising castling as soon as feasible to insure king safety.
   Unfortunately, it can't be applied indiscriminately. There are plenty of times when you should delay castling or not castle at all. Probably a better principle would be to *prepare* to castle—to get the *ability* to castle—fairly quickly, just in case castling suddenly becomes desirable or necessary.

Castle into Check   A violation of the rules. The king may never move into check.

Castle Kingside   To castle using the king-rook. The move is written "0-0." Also called CASTLE SHORT.

Castle Long   To CASTLE QUEENSIDE.

Castle on Opposite Sides White castles on the queenside and Black on the kingside, or Black on the queenside and White on the kingside.

It's often recommended by teachers to develop attacking skills. Students castle on opposite sides and advance pawns against the enemy king to create tactical opportunities.

Castle out of Check A violation of the rules.

A king in check must get out of check without castling. If the king doesn't move, it may be able to castle later.

Castle Queenside To castle using the queen-rook. The move is written "0-0-0." Also called CASTLE LONG.

Castle Short To CASTLE KINGSIDE.

Castle Through Check In the act of castling, to move the king over a square guarded by the enemy, a violation of the rules even though the king doesn't stop on this attacked square.

Castling Playing the king and rook on the same move, which is the only time two pieces can be moved on the same turn. Castling is possible on either the kingside or the queenside. It is achieved by transferring the king two squares toward the rook (to the g-file if castling kingside, to the c-file if castling queenside) and then putting the rook on the square next to the king on its other side.

Castling is permitted only if certain conditions are met. The intervening squares between the king and castling rook must be unoccupied. Both the king and the rook must not have moved in the game. You can't castle if you're in check (it is legal, however, to castle on a subsequent move if the king hasn't moved) or if the king must pass through check (over a square guarded by the opponent), or if the king is in check after completing castling.

Casual Game An offhand or friendly game played for entertainment. See SKITTLES.

Center The four squares in the very middle of the board, namely d4, d5, e5, and e4. Also the region containing this block of four as well as the twelve squares surrounding it: c3, c4, c5, c6, d6, e6, f6, f5, f4, f3, e3, and d3.

Central Of the center; concerning the middle of the board.

Centralization In the opening and middlegame, a principle recommending the development of pieces toward the center for general readiness. In the endgame, the process of bringing the king and other pieces back to the center before commencing certain plans or campaigns.

Centralize To move toward the center, usually to prepare for critical or final stages.

Central Zone The area contained within the square c6 to f6 to f3 to c3. Also called ENLARGED CENTER.

Centurini's Position A famous ending of king, bishop, and knight-pawn vs. king and bishop, in which an elaborate bishop maneuver gains a TEMPO and wins.

W: Kc8 Bg3 Pb7 (3)
B: Kc6 Ba7 (2)

QUESTION: What tactic enables White to promote his pawn?

Centurini's actual starting position (W: Kc8 Bd8 Pb7 B: Kc6 Bh2) leads to the diagram after 1. Bh4 Kb6 2. Bf2+ Ka7 3. Bc5 Bg3 4. Be7 Kb6 5. Bd8+ Kc6 6. Bh4! Bh2 7. Bf2 Bf4 8. Ba7 Bh2 9. Bb8 Bg1 10. Bg3 Ba7.

ANSWER: White wins by a deflection, 11. Bf2. If Black takes White's bishop, the pawn queens. Otherwise, White simply captures Black's bishop and promotes after that.

Chaturanga The earliest known forerunner of chess, which appears to have originated in the fifth century A.D. in the Indus Valley.

Chain Short for PAWN CHAIN.

Cheapo Slang for an on obvious trap or one-move setup. See
SUCKER PUNCH.

Check A direct attack or threat to the king.

When one of your units checks the opposing king, you are in position to capture the king on the next move (though the rules actually prevent a king from being captured). A king "in check" must get "out of check" immediately.

Checking Distance The minimum distance a rook needs to attack without being in danger of counterattack from the approaching enemy king.

W: Kd8 Rc2 Pd7   (3)
B: Kb7 Rh2   (2)

QUESTION: Can Black play to draw?

In most cases the rook has the checking distance if it's at least four squares from its target along the line of attack. The target is either the enemy king, a passed pawn, or the complex of both. If the rook is only three squares away, the opposing king may be able to chase the rook without endangering the pawn, which can then proceed toward promotion.

ANSWER: Black's rook has the checking distance from the flank, allowing it to pester the White king into a draw. A reasonable variation is 1. . . . Rh8+ 2. Ke7 Rh7+ 3. Ke6 Rh6+ 4. Kf7 Rh7+, forcing the king back to the pawn's defense. Worse is 4. Kf5, when 4. . . . Rd6 wins the pawn.

Checkmate   A situation in which an attacked king has no legal way to get out of check. The game ends at this point, before the check-mated king is actually captured. (If the rules permitted it, the king would be taken on the next turn.)

Chessboard   The playing surface, which is a square board consist-ing of 64 smaller squares, 32 light and 32 dark, arranged in an alternat-ing pattern. At the start the board is placed with a light square in the corner to each player's right.

Chess by Mail   See CORRESPONDENCE CHESS.

Chess Clock   A timing device with two clocks, one for White and one for Black.

When it's your move, your time runs and your opponent's doesn't. After completing your move, you can stop your clock and start your opponent's. Then it's your opponent's turn to move and, after mov-ing, he stops his clock and starts yours.

Chessmaster   See NATIONAL MASTER.

Chessmen   Pieces and pawns considered as a group. See UNITS.

Chess Problem   See PROBLEM.

Circuit In certain knight endings, a circular path of four squares connected by knight moves.

W: Kg6 Ph6 (2)
B: Ka1 Ng5 (2)

QUESTION: Can Black move and draw?

If the defending knight can get on the circuit it can stop the pawn from safely advancing. In the diagram the circuit consists of the squares h7, f8, e6, and g5. Although the knight must move, it can stay on the circuit and draw.

ANSWER: The position is held by 1. . . . Ne6!, when 2. h7 encounters 2. . . . Nf8+ 3. Kg7 Nxh7 4. Kxh7, and the game is drawn due to INSUFFICIENT MATING MATERIAL.

Classical Pertaining to a style favoring straightforward play, including direct occupation of the center, especially with pawns; rapid development; early castling; and adherence to standard principles. Also, the style itself.

Classical Pawn Center Aligned center pawns on a player's fourth rank. For White, pawns on d4 and e4; for Black, pawns on d5 and e5.

This is called a classical pawn center because such a formation was the aim of the early generations of good players in the 17th and 18th centuries. They laid down the "classical principles" in their games and analyses.

Classic Bishop Sacrifice See GRECO'S SACRIFICE.

Clean Mate A problem composition term. A mate in which unoccupied squares near the mated king are each guarded only once, none of the units in the pattern have unnecessary functions, and the mating move is not a double check. Also called PURE MATE. See MODEL MATE.

Clear Unblocked, as a clear line. Also, definite, as a clear advantage.

Clearance A tactic by which a square or line is evacuated, typically by a compelling sacrifice, so that a friendly unit can occupy the same square or line. See ANNIHILATION.

W: Ka1 Qa6 Bb1 Pa2   (4)
B: Kh8 Rb5 Ba7 Nd4   (4)

QUESTION: How can Black mate in two moves?

Annihilation is a form of clearance. But whereas clearance is the unblocking of either a square or line, annihilation refers specifically to a line.

ANSWER: Black mates by the sacrifice 1. . . . Nc2+. After 2. Bxc2, Black's bishop mates on d4, the square just cleared by the knight.

Clearance Sacrifice See CLEARANCE.

Clock See CHESS CLOCK.

Clock Game A game using a chess clock to make sure the players complete a certain number of moves in a specified period. A player failing to make the TIME CONTROL forfeits the game.

Closed Center A center blocked by chains of black and white pawns. Loosely, any center through which movement is hindered by pawns.

A typical closed center has white pawns at d5 and e4 interlocked with black pawns at d6 and e5; or white pawns at d4 and e5 versus black pawns at d5 and e6. When the middle of the board is obstructed by pawns, play tends to take place behind the lines, around the perimeter of the center, or on the flanks. The action is correspondingly slower, since it's harder to transfer pieces through the central barricade, and intricate maneuvers are common. It's not unusual to see knights, with their ability to pirouette, get the better of bishops. Finally, the blocked center often enables the kings to remain uncastled into the early middlegame and even beyond in preparation for transition to the endgame. See PAWN CHAIN, ATTACK AT THE BASE OF THE PAWN CHAIN, CLOSED GAME, and FIXED PAWNS.

Closed File A file occupied by both white and black pawns, so that rooks and queens cannot move along it completely. See OPEN FILE and HALF-OPEN FILE.

Close Game Another name for CLOSED GAME.

Closed Game One with a CLOSED CENTER (obstructed by white and black pawns), in which few, if any, exchanges have taken place. Also called CLOSE GAME or CLOSED POSITION.

Closed Opening A game that begins with 1. d4, or sometimes 1. c4. Also called CLOSE OPENING.

Queen-pawn openings, in contrast to those beginning with the king-pawn, are more likely to produce closed games if played automatically. But they are conducted so actively these days, and with such vigor and creativity, that the distinction has become more a convenience of classification than a reliable rule of thumb.

Closed Position See CLOSED GAME.

Coffeehouse Chess A type of chess typical of coffeehouses, characterized by risky unsound play that in those circumstances (noisy, smoky, confused) can be difficult to refute.

Color Weakness A difficulty in adequately guarding, occupying, or influencing squares of one color.

W: Kd1 Bd5 Ps b3 d3 f5 h6   (6)
B: Kf8 Bb6 Ps b4 d6 e5 f6   (6)

QUESTION: Can White force a win?

A color weakness tends to be pronounced when one's pawns are fixed on squares of the other color and one's minor pieces are powerless to help. A balancing act occurs with opposite-color bishops, when both players may be weak and strong on different color squares. It all depends on circumstances.

ANSWER: Black can't stop a white king trek to g6 (Kd1-e2-f3-g4-h5-g6) and the subsequent pawn advance h6-h7.

Column Another name for FILE.

Combination A sequence of forced moves, usually involving sacrifice, always leading to an improvement of one's situation.

W: Kg1 Qa6 Bg2 Ng6 Ps f2 g3   (6)
B: Kg8 Qa8 Bd6 Nh7 Ps a7 c7 d5 g7 (8)

QUESTION: Does White have a winning combination?

The word "combination" implies a synthesis of several tactical themes. The usual aims are checkmate or gain of material. A true combination requires sacrifice, but of a particular kind. Combinative sacrifices work by force. They are not REAL SACRIFICES, where the outcome is in doubt, but SHAM SACRIFICES, where favorable results have been foreseen.

ANSWER: After 1. Qc8 + ! Black must abandon his queen, for 1. . . . Qxc8 allows 2. Bxd5 + and mate next move.

Companion Squares Also called CONJUGATE SQUARES, COORDINATE SQUARES, CORRESPONDING SQUARES, RELATED SQUARES, and SISTER SQUARES. See THEORY OF CORRESPONDING SQUARES.

Compensation A counterbalancing advantage to offset one or more disadvantages.

The term is based on a comparison of different elements, such as material vs. time. A player might have an extra pawn to compensate for the opponent's initiative. It's also possible to have compensation within the same element, such as material. One side gets a knight, for example, for his opponent's three pawns.

Complicate To keep the position complex by avoiding trades and retaining tension; to initiate risky, hard-to-analyze lines, possibly involving sacrifice.

Complications Unanticipated difficulties or tactics that confuse and jeopardize the outcome.

Composed Problem A deliberately created position, not necessarily reflecting a real game situation, that sets out in a clever or artistic way a particular technique or theme. Like puzzles, they are meant to be solved. A problem often must be solved in a specified number of moves. See COMPOSITION, PROBLEM, and STUDY.

W: Kg1 Qh8 Rh7 Pa6 (4)
B: Ka8 Bb8 Ps a7 g2 (4)

QUESTION: How does White force mate in two moves?

In an artfully composed problem everything meshes perfectly, nothing is wasted, every unit has a definite purpose, and, ideally, there is only one answer. Alternative solutions, known as cooks, mar the problem.

ANSWER: In this version of a famous problem composed by Sam Loyd (1841-1911), White mates by 1. Rh1!, followed by 2. Qxh1#.

Composition A COMPOSED PROBLEM or STUDY. See COOK.

All kinds of creations may be considered compositions, including forced mates, endgame studies, tasks, instructional examples, mathematical/logical puzzles, chess jokes, and who knows what. Some of these are quite fantastic, having unusual stipulations and bearing little resemblance to actual competition.

Computer Notation   The barest form of algebraic notation, giving only the moving unit's starting and destination squares.

Piece symbols are not used, nor are there indications for captures or checks. For example, if a White knight on e4 captures a Black knight on f6, giving check, the move is simply written "e4-f6" or "E4-F6."

Concrete Advantage   A tangible advantage, like material or pawn structure, that tends to be long-lasting.

Conditional Problem   A kind of problem in which standard pieces have enhanced or restricted powers.

Conflicting Principles   General guidelines that seem to disagree.

An example is being ahead by a pawn with a powerful attack and having the opportunity to trade pieces. One principle recommends exchanging when ahead, the other says to avoid trades if pressing an attack. What do you do? Try thinking and figuring out what's really best.

Conjugate Square   Also called COMPANION SQUARES, COORDINATE SQUARES, CORRESPONDING SQUARES, RELATED SQUARES, and SISTER SQUARES. See THEORY OF CORRESPONDING SQUARES.

Connected   For pieces, occupying the same line and capable of supporting each other (see CONNECTING THE ROOKS); for pawns, occupying adjacent files and capable of defending each other (see CONNECTED PASSED PAWNS).

Connected Passed Pawns   Two friendly passed pawns on adjacent files. See PASSED PAWN.

W: Kf3 Ps a7 b5   (3)
B: Kb7   (1)

QUESTION: How does White win this ending?

Connected passed pawns are often a vital endgame weapon because they can advance with mutual support. When one of them is placed to protect the other, the opposing king can't capture the protecting back pawn without allowing the protected front one to run toward promotion.

ANSWER: White secures the day by 1. b6. A possible conclusion is 1. . . . Ka8 2. Kf4 Kb7 3. Ke5 Ka8 4. Kd6 Kb7 5. a8/Q+ Kxa8 6. Kc6 Kb8 7. b7 Ka7 8. Kc7 Ka6 9. b8/Q Ka5 10. Qb3 Ka6 11. Qa4# (or 11. Qb6#).

Connecting the Rooks   Clearing the home rank by developing the queen and minor pieces and castling, so that the rooks defend each other. The situation signifies a state of readiness and usually marks the end of the opening and the start of the middlegame.

Consolidate To stabilize a loose or uncoordinated position.

One usually consolidates with several defensive or simplifying moves, exchanging off menacing or clumsy pieces while completing development and safeguarding the king. The concept most often applies after risking the win of material or surviving an intense period of attack.

Consolidation The process of stabilizing and refocusing a position, especially after a period of activity, by insuring king safety, defending weak points, completing development, repositioning certain pieces, and warding off potential enemy threats.

Consultation Game A game in which two or more players work as a team, discussing their moves before playing them. The opponent may be a single player or another consultation team.

Continuation A follow-up to a move or series of moves.

Convergent Thinking In chess, working out the precise moves when we already know what to do. It is linear and one-dimensional, as opposed to DIVERGENT THINKING.

Cook In composed problems, an alternative solution, often requiring fewer moves, usually missed by the composer. A cook spoils the validity of a composition.

Coordinate Notation Any notation that views the board as a coordinate grid, such as ALGEBRAIC NOTATION.

Coordinate Squares Also called COMPANION SQUARES, CONJUGATE SQUARES, CORRESPONDING SQUARES, RELATED SQUARES, and SISTER SQUARES. See THEORY OF CORRESPONDING SQUARES.

Cordon In the endgame, a boundary line, consisting of guarded squares and sometimes the board's edge, that confines a king within a particular area.

Corral The trapping of a knight by a bishop along the edge. Also referred to as CORRALLING A KNIGHT.

W: Kd7 Bh2 Pg2 (3)
B: Ka7 Nh5 Pa6 (3)

QUESTION: How does White win?

This is one reason to avoid positioning a knight along the board's perimeter. A knight has such reduced mobility there that a smartly placed bishop can usurp all of its possible moves.

ANSWER: After 1. Be5!, the knight is helpless against the pending advance g2-g4.

Correspondence Chess Chess played by mailing each move in a letter or on a postcard.

Correspondence chess requires a real investment in time. In today's high-tech age, where information is conveyed immediately by telephone, fax, or computer modems, it may have seen its day.

Corresponding Squares   Also called COMPANION SQUARES, CONJU-
GAL SQUARES, COORDINATE SQUARES, RELATED SQUARES, and SISTER SQUARES. See
THEORY OF CORRESPONDING SQUARES.

Corridor Mate   A line mate by a rook or queen, given along any
file or rank when possible escape squares are guarded or obstructed.
See BACK-RANK MATE.

Counter   An answer or response. See COUNTERATTACK.

Counterattack   An attack mounted by the defender or the player
apparently on the defensive. Also, one of a certain class of opening
variations initiated by Black.

A good counterattacker adequately answers the opponent's threats
while generating some of his own. It's a mistake just to strike out
blindly, however ferociously. You can't ignore enemy plans, even if
they seem trivial or unimportant, especially when they come first.

Counterchances   Opportunities for COUNTERATTACK.

Countergambit   Generally, an opening gambit offered by Black
in response to White's opening gambit; thus, an attempt to seize the
initiative and blunt White's attack.

Counterplay   The possibility for the defending side to undertake
aggressive action, usually by opening another front. A player who has
counterplay is said to have overall chances roughly equal to the
opponent's.

Counting   With regard to material, comparing pieces and pawns
to see who's ahead; with regard to pawn races, determining which

side promotes first; with regard to maneuvers, especially for the king, figuring how many moves it takes to reach a certain square.

Cramped
Constricted; especially, blocked or restrained by pawns that fix one's pawns to the third rank, leaving very little room for positioning behind the lines.

Cramped Position
A position in which one side in particular has reduced space.

Crippled Majority
A pawn majority incapable of producing a candidate, usually because of doubled or isolated pawns.

Critical Diagonal of Retreat
In pawn endings, the shortest path for the defending king to the promotion square; the diagonal the king needs to traverse to stop the pawn from queening.

W: Kf1 Ps a2 d4   (3)

B: Kf3 Ps e6 f7   (3)

QUESTION: How does White play and win?

A key battle often revolves around the attacker's attempt at blocking a critical diagonal, preventing the defending king's auspicious retreat.

ANSWER: White wins by blocking the diagonal line with a pawn sacrifice, 1. d5!, and after 1. . . . exd5 2. a4 d4 3. a5 d3 4. Ke1, there's no catching the a-pawn.

Critical Opposition In endgame theory, the opposition allowing a king to occupy a critical square. See OPPOSITION and THEORY OF CRITICAL SQUARES. Also called KEY OPPOSITION.

Critical Position That point in a theoretically important line, usually in the opening and more or less forced from the preceding moves, the evaluation of which determines whether the sequence favors White or Black. Also, any decisive turning point in a game.

Critical Square A square whose occupation by the superior side's king insures the completion of a task. An endgame concept.

Critical Thinking Abstract reasoning used to solve problems; higher thought processes marked by careful analysis and evaluation of alternatives before deciding on the optimal course of action. See ANALOGUE and LATERAL THINKING.

Cross-Check A check that blocks a check by the opponent.

W: Ka8 Qf4   (2)
B: Kf2 Qd3 Pe2   (3)

QUESTION: How does Black end the checks?

In addition to cross-checking by interposition, it is possible to move the king and discover check or to capture the checking unit with check. The most typical cross-checking situation occurs in queen endings to avoid perpetual check.

ANSWER: Black wins by 1. . . . Qf3 +, blocking check with check and forcing a trade of queens. The pawn then promotes.

Crossover A maneuver by a king in front of and across the path of one of its own passed pawns to reach the OUTSIDE CRITICAL SQUARE. Also called the OVERPASS, in contrast to the UNDERPASS.

W: Kf3 Pd4 (2)
B: Kg7 (1)

QUESTION: How does White insure the pawn's promotion?

White's king must get to any of the pawn's three critical squares to guide the pawn home. In this situation, with the passed pawn on its fourth rank, the critical squares are c6, d6, and e6.

ANSWER: A direct diagonal crossover to c6 does the job: 1. Ke4 Kf6 2. Kd5 Ke7 3. Kc6. A possible finish is 3. . . . Kd8 4. d5 Kc8 5. d6 Kd8 6. d7 Ke7 7. Kc7 and the pawn promotes next move.

Cross-Pin   A counter-pin. Answering a pin with a pin.

W: Kh1 Rb1 Bf1 Nc6 Ps e6 h5   (6)
B: Kc8 Rh8 Bb7 Nh4 Ps a6 c7 c5   (7)

QUESTION: How does White mate in two moves?

The cross-pin idea is more prevalent in problem composition, though it does arise in ordinary play as well, especially in situations needing a defensive fix.

ANSWER: White's 1. Bxa6! cross-pins Black's bishop (which is pinning White's knight) to its king and mates next move. If 1. . . . Bxa6, then 2. Rb8#. Otherwise, White's bishop captures on b7, giving mate with support from the rook.

Crosstable A chart or table showing the results of every player in a tournament.

	Einstein	Freud	Darwin	Twain	WL
Albert Einstein	✕	1	½	1	2½–½
Sigmund Freud	0	✕	½	1	1½–1½
Charles Darwin	½	½	✕	1	2–1
Mark Twain	0	0	0	✕	0–3

Cutoff A queen, rook, or bishop barrier that the opposing king can't cross.

W: Kh8 Rg8   (2)
B: Kb6 Pa5   (2)

QUESTION: How does White force a win?

Cutoffs tend to be most valuable in rook endings, where it becomes necessary to prevent the opposing king from supporting or trying to stop a passed pawn's advance. The cutoff should be maintained until the last possible moment to give your own forces a chance to join the fray.

ANSWER: White wins by cutting off the Black king with 1. Rg5!, when Black is dead after 1. . . . a4 2. Kg7 a3 3. Rg3 a2 4. Ra3.

D

Dance of Death A phrase capturing the spirit of the oppositional fight between two kings. See OPPOSITION.

Dangerous Diagonal Either of the two diagonals on which the FOOL'S MATE can occur. White can be so mated along the e1-h4 diagonal, Black along the e8-h5 diagonal.

Dark-Square Bishop A bishop that moves only on dark squares. For White, the queenside bishop starting on c1; for Black, the kingside bishop starting on f8.

Dark-Square Game An opening plan to control the dark squares. A type of game with this theme.

If you're playing a dark-square game, try to control especially the squares on the a1-h8 diagonal, which come under the influence of the dark-square bishops. When both sides have developed their kingside bishops on the flank (White's at g2, Black's at g7), Black is equipped for a dark-square game and White for a light-square one. A typical dark-square setup for Black has a bishop at g7, a knight at c6, and pawns on c5, d6, and e7. A similar scheme for White offers a bishop on b2, a knight on f3, and pawns on d2, e3, and f4.

Dark Squares The 32 squares of the same color as a1. Also called black squares, even if they're not black.

Decoy A distant pawn offered as a sacrifice to lure an enemy piece (usually the king) out of position. See OUTSIDE PASSED PAWN and DEFLECTION.

W: Ke3 Ps c3 h4 (3)
B: Ke5 Ps b5 c4 (3)

QUESTION: How should White continue?

A decoy becomes more valuable the farther it is from the main sector of dispute, especially when the only defender is the enemy king.

ANSWER: White should play 1. h5. After 1. . . . Kf5 2. Kd4 Kg5 3. Kc5 Kxh5 4. Kxb5 Kg5 5. Kxc4 White wins the ending.

Deductive Reasoning   In chess, the mental process of proceeding logically from one or more related ideas to a goal that seems to follow necessarily. This is what chessplayers do, for example, when they analyze forcing variations that lead to mate or other definite positions that can be understood and evaluated with certainty. See INDUCTIVE REASONING.

Defender   The player under attack. At the start of the game, White is the attacker and Black the defender. Also, any unit that protects another unit.

Defense   A move or series of moves designed to meet opposing threats and attacks, whether immediate or long range. In the openings, a defense is a system of play whose characteristic positions are determined largely by Black.

Deflection   Forcing an enemy unit from its post, leaving a certain square or set of squares inadequately guarded. See DECOY.

Demo Board   Short for DEMONSTRATION BOARD.

Demonstration Board   A large chessboard with movable pieces, mounted upright for display and instruction.

Derivative   Not original; usually said of opening ideas developed by others.

Descriptive Notation   A system of notating moves in which every square has two names depending on whose move it is. For example, P-K4 when played by White is a pawn advance from e2 to e4; when played by Black it's a pawn move from e7 to e5. The algebraic system is preferred today. See ALGEBRAIC NOTATION.

Desperado A tactic by which a threatened or trapped piece is sacrificed to minimize loss, inflict damage, or gain material.

W: Ka1 Qd5 Bh2 Ps a2 b3 (5)
B: Ke8 Qa3 Be6 Ps d7 f7 (5)

QUESTION: Who wins?

Sometimes desperado possibilities arise when, instead of extricating an attacked piece, you let it hang and threaten a comparable piece of the opponent's. The player who goes first in such circumstances has a great advantage because of the possibility of getting something for the attacked piece with a gain of time, while the opponent gets nothing.

ANSWER: Whoever moves wins by sacrificing the queen for the opponent's bishop and then capturing the other side's queen.

Develop To improve a piece's scope or potential, or both, by moving it to a better square or by moving something, especially a pawn, out of its way. In the opening, to move a piece off its home rank or shift a rook to an unblocked file.

Developing Sacrifice A sacrifice to gain time for development. See SACRIFICE.

Development The process of increasing the mobility of pieces by moving them from their original squares to more active ones or by moving pawns out of their way. In the opening it usually implies moving pieces, other than rooks, off their home rank. Rooks are developed when placed on open, half-open, or about-to-open files.

Develop Toward the Center A maxim advising players to develop pieces toward the middle in the opening.

Diagonal A slanted row of same-colored squares. There are 26 different diagonals on the chessboard. See BISHOP.

Diagonal March A maneuver enabling a king to approach two widely separated squares simultaneously by traveling along a diagonal that is equidistant from both.

W: Ka3 Ph4 (2)
B: Kh1 Pc3 (2)

QUESTION: If it's Black's move, can Black draw?

The diagram is a famous endgame study composed by Richard Reti. Black's king can't catch the h-pawn, nor can it get over in time to defend the black c-pawn; but by threatening both Black can save the game.

ANSWER: Black draws with a diagonal march: 1. . . . Kg2 2. h5 Kf3 3. Kb3 Ke4! 4. h6 Kd3 5. h7 c2 6. h8/Q c1/Q, and White's checks are useless; or 3. h6 Ke2 4. h7 c2 and draws.

Diagonal Opposition
An opposition in which the kings are separated by one, three, or five squares along the same diagonal. It includes diagonal opposition (one square in between the two kings), distant diagonal opposition (three square in between), and long-distant diagonal opposition (five squares in between). See OPPOSITION.

Diagram
A pictorial representation of the chessboard and pieces. The white pieces usually start at the bottom and the black at the top.

Didactic Position
A position used for instruction. It could be created, adapted, or taken from real play.

Direct Attack
The placement of a unit in position to capture another with advantage.

Direct Opposition
An opposition in which the kings are separated by one square on a file, rank, or diagonal. Direct vertical opposition is along a file, direct horizontal opposition is along a rank, direct diagonal opposition is along a diagonal. See OPPOSITION.

Direct Protection
Guarding a unit by moving another one into position to recapture.

Discovered Attack
An attack by a piece created when a friendly piece moves out of its way. This often results in two simultaneous

attacks: one from the stationary unit and one from the moving one. Also called DISCOVERY.

Discovered Check
A discovery in which the stationary attacker gives check. See DISCOVERED ATTACK.

W: Kg4 Rd4 Ba5 Pf5   (4)

B: Ke5   (1)

QUESTION: How can White force mate in two moves?

A discovered check can be quite potent. While the defender must take the time to get out of the stationary unit's check, the moving unit has virtual carte blanche, capturing and threatening with abandon.

ANSWER: It's mate after 1. Bc3 Kf6 2. Rd7#. Here the moving unit is used to close the door.

Discovery
Another name for DISCOVERED ATTACK.

Distant Diagonal Opposition
A diagonal opposition in which the kings are separated by three or five squares. See OPPOSITION.

Distant Opposition An opposition in which the kings are separated by three or five squares on a file, rank, or diagonal. Distant horizontal opposition is along a file, distant vertical opposition is along a rank, and distant diagonal opposition is along a diagonal. See OPPOSITION.

Divergent Thinking In chess, multidimensional thinking, not bound by circumstances, open to sudden shifts in context and viewpoint, and drawing upon unexpected moves and resources creatively to solve complex problems. Also called LATERAL THINKING. See CONVERGENT THINKING.

Domination In endgame studies, a tactic by which a piece is trapped and won by a combination of direct attack and other, indirect, methods that take away all flight squares.

Double To put two pieces of like power on the same line. To form a BATTERY. For example, to double rooks on a file.

Double Attack Two or more attacks stemming from the same move. Usually, a simultaneous attack against two separate targets either by one unit against two (a FORK) or by two against two (a DISCOVERY).

Double-Bishop Sacrifice See TWO-BISHOP SACRIFICE.

Double Bughouse Another name for BUGHOUSE.

Double Check A discovery in which both the moving and stationary attackers give check.

W: Kg1 Qe2 Ne4 Pg2   (4)
B: Ke8 Qd8 Bf3 Nf8 Pf7   (5)

QUESTION: How should White take the bishop on f3?

Double check is often described as the most powerful move in chess. The only way to get out of it is to move the king.

ANSWER: Why take the bishop? You can mate in one move with 1. Nf6#.

Double Fianchetto An opening or defense in which a player develops both bishops on the flanks.

Doubled Isolated Pawns Two pawns of the same color on the same file, neither of which is capable of being defended by a pawn because no friendly pawns occupy adjacent files.

Doubled Pawns Two friendly pawns occupying the same file and therefore incapable of protecting each other.

Doubled Rooks Two rooks on the same rank or file. A BATTERY.

Double Leap For each pawn, the initial possibility of moving two squares.

Double-Rook Sacrifice The sacrifice of two rooks to exact mate at the other end. See IMMORTAL GAME.

Double Threat Two different simultaneous threats, not necessarily of the same type or given by the same unit. See DOUBLE ATTACK.

W: Kf5 Ra3 Rc2   (3)
B: Kd1 Qh4   (2)

QUESTION: How can White force a win?

Most double attacks are really simple forks given by one unit. But a double threat can be another story, involving several friendly units and radically different tactics.

ANSWER: White wins with 1. Rh2!, which sets up the double threat of taking the queen and mating at a1. If 1. . . . Qd4 (1. . . . Qxh2 2. Ra1 + Ke2 3. Ra2 + skewers king and queen) 2. Ra1 + ! Qxa1 3. Rh1 + , winning the queen after all.

Doubling   Placing two major pieces on the same rank or file or a queen and bishop on the same diagonal.

Down   Behind, as in material. Also, toward the enemy, as in "down the board."

Down the Exchange   Having only a minor piece against the opponent's rook.

Down a Pawn   Behind by a pawn. Having one less pawn than the opponent.

Down a Piece   Behind by a knight or a bishop, not by a queen or a rook, which would be specifically indicated ("down a rook").

Draw   A chess game that is not won by either player. There are five ways to draw: agreement, threefold repetition, 50-move rule, insufficient mating material, and stalemate. In tournament or match competition each player receives half a point for drawing.

Draw by Agreement   A draw in which one player proposes a draw and the other accepts.

Draw by Insufficient Mating Material   See INSUFFICIENT MATING MATERIAL.

Draw by Perpetual Check   See PERPETUAL CHECK.

Draw by Repetition   A draw by repeating the same position (not the same move) on three separate occasions, not necessarily consecutive. The draw must be claimed by the player before making the move that brings about the third repetition. See REPETITION OF POSITION RULE and THREEFOLD REPETITION.

Draw by Stalemate   See STALEMATE.

Draw by the 50-Move Rule   See 50-MOVE RULE.

Draw by Threefold Repetition   See THREEFOLD REPETITION.

Drawing Chance   A possibility to save a lost game.

Drawn Game   A game ending in a draw. See DRAWN POSITION.

Drawn Position   A position in which neither player has real chances to win. The game should end in a draw if both play the best moves.

Dresden Stonewall   A type of Stonewall setup, with white pawns at c4, d3, and e4 vs. black pawns at c5, d6, and e5. Compare to the DUTCH STONEWALL.

Dresden Stonewall Formation   See DRESDEN STONEWALL.

Driving Back   Forcing a retreat, often by attacking with a pawn.

Driving Off   Another name for DEFLECTION.

Driving On   Another name for ATTRACTION.

Duffer   A weak player. See FISH.

Dutch Stonewall   The typical Stonewall setup, with white pawns at d4, e3, and f4 vs. black pawns at d5, e6, and f5. See STONEWALL.

Dutch Stonewall Formation   See DUTCH STONEWALL.

Dynamic   Active; with mobile forces.

Dynamic Center   A pawn center with tension or that hasn't yet assumed definite form. It could become any of four different centers: an OPEN CENTER, CLOSED CENTER, FIXED CENTER, or MOBILE CENTER.

Dynamic Factors   Elements that contribute to attack, including time (initiative and development), mobility, control of open lines and key squares, and healthy pawns capable of vigorous advance.

Dynamics   All aspects of movement and attack taken together.

E

Echo The recurrence of the same or a similar theme in a single game. In problem composition, the purposeful imitation of a certain theme in different variations of the same problem, not necessarily by the same color. Commonly, the purposeful or incidental occurrence of the same idea in any two chess situations.

Eclectic With regard to opening repertoire and style, selecting and playing dissimilar lines that have no common thread for the sake of variety and interest.

Economy The achievement of a task with minimum effort and resources. In problem composition, the use of the least amount of force necessary to accomplish the goal with no superfluous material on the board, a necessary ingredient of artistry.

Edge   Any of the board's four outside rows: the a-file, the eighth rank, the h-file, or the first rank. Also, an advantage.

Eighth Rank   In algebraic notation, the rank occupied by Black's pieces in the original position. In descriptive notation, the rank occupied by the opponent's pieces at the game's start.

Eight-Queens Problem   A famous chess puzzle. The solver must place eight queens on an empty chessboard so that no queen is in position to capture any other. One of the 92 solutions: queens on b1, d2, f3, h4, a6, c5, e8, and g7.

Element   A constituent of the overall advantage; one of its aspects. See ELEMENTS.

Elements   The factors that determine which side has the advantage. There are many elements, but the five fundamental ones are SPACE, TIME, PAWN STRUCTURE, MATERIAL, and KING SAFETY.

Elo Rating   A method of rating chessplayers developed by Professor Arpad Elo of the United States. FIDE uses a slightly modified form of it for its international tournaments and matches. Also called FIDE RATING.

Endgame   The final phase of a chess game, after the opening and middlegame. See ENDING.

Ending   Another name for ENDGAME, but it also refers to a specific endgame position.

Enemy   The opponent, but it's also used adjectivally as in "enemy attack" or "enemy position."

Enlarged Center An area consisting of the four middle squares, d4, d5, e4, and e5, plus the 12 squares surrounding them: c3, c4, c5, c6, d6, e6, f6, f5, f4, f3, e3, and d3. It can't hurt to dominate this region.

En Passant A type of pawn capture. If a pawn is already on its fifth rank, and an enemy pawn on an adjacent file advances two squares so that both pawns occupy the same rank, the first pawn may capture the second as if it had moved only one square. The option must be exercised on the first opportunity or not at all.

Enveloping Attack An attack from behind the enemy forces.

Enveloping Maneuver A redeployment of a piece, either from the front or flank, to a more aggressive position in the rear.

Epaulet Mate A mate by a queen or rook, in which two possible escape squares, to the immediate left and right of the mated king, are blocked by the king's own forces. The losing king is usually mated on the edge of the board.

W: Kh2 Qc7 Rh1 Ps g2 h3   (5)
B: Kg8 Qe3 Rf3 Pg7   (4)

QUESTION: How should Black save his rook?

An epaulet (or epaulette) is the French word for the ornamental shoulder piece on certain military uniforms. In the epaulet mate, the blocking pieces evoke that image.

ANSWER: Don't save the rook. Instead, throw it away to rip open the seventh rank for an epaulet mate: 1. . . . Rxh3 + ! 2. gxh3 Qf2#.

En Prise "In take." A French term indicating an undefended unit in position to be captured.

Equal Even in material and having approximately the same chances of winning as the opponent.

Equality A situation in which both sides have roughly the same chances to win.

Equalize To reach a position of dynamic equilibrium and/or material equality with more or less the same winning chances.

Equilibrium A balanced position, in which each side's advantages offset the opponent's and both players have comparable attacking and counterattacking chances. Disturbing the equilibrium can be very risky.

Error A mistake, but not quite as bad as a blunder. Loosely, any faulty play, whether it loses or merely lets slip the advantage: an oversight, miscalculation, misjudgment, getting into time-trouble, not taking the opponent seriously, etc.

Escape Square A square to which the king could flee in avoidance of mate, especially against back-rank threats.

W: Ke6 Ra8 Ne8   (3)
B: Kg8 Rg7 Bb2   (3)

QUESTION: Should the knight take the rook?

When an escape hatch is created for a castled king by advancing a pawn, the player is "making LUFT."

ANSWER: No way. Forget the rook. Mate by 1. Nf6#. The knight check usurps the h7 escape square.

Evaluation In chess analysis, judging or determining the worth of a move, variation, plan, or position.

Even Exchange See EVEN TRADE.

Even Game A game with no material or positional advantages for either side.

Even Position Essentially the same as EVEN GAME.

Even Trade An exchange of comparable material, such as a queen for a queen, a rook for a rook, or a minor piece for a minor piece. Also, the exchange of dissimilar material of equivalent values, such as a bishop for three pawns, or a rook for a knight and two pawns.

Exchange An equal trade; also, to trade equal amounts of material. THE EXCHANGE, however, is the difference in value between a rook and a minor piece, as in "to win the exchange."

Exchange Down Behind by the exchange. Having only a minor piece for a rook. Also, to trade.

Exchange Sacrifice To sacrifice a rook for a bishop or knight. See RUSSIAN EXCHANGE SACRIFICE.

W: Kg1 Qc4 Rf1 Bc2 Ps d4 g2 h3   (7)
B: Kh8 Qb7 Rf8 Nf6 Ps c6 c7 f7 g7   (8)

QUESTION: How should White push the attack?

Exchange sacrifices are not uncommon with the defending queen removed from play. Sometimes you have to be daring.

ANSWER: White should sacrifice the exchange, 1. Rxf6! gxf6, and follow with 2. Qd3, menacing mate at h7. A possible conclusion is 2. . . . f5 3. Qxf5 Kg7 4. Qg5+ Kh8 5. Qh6+ Kg8 6. Qh7#.

Exchange Values The relative values of pieces and pawns; a pawn is worth one pawn, a bishop or knight three pawns, a rook five, and a queen nine. Also called RELATIVE VALUES OF THE PIECES.

Exhibition A game or set of games played for public presentation and entertainment and not for professional advancement or qualification. See SIMULTANEOUS EXHIBITION.

Exhibition Game A game without official sanction played for public display and not usually governed by strict tournament rules.

Exhibition Match A game or series of games played between two players, possibly for stakes, but not for official distinctions or titles. Also, a similar confrontation between teams.

Exposed King Generally, a king without proper pawn shields and therefore subject to attack. Also, a king in an open center and unable to find shelter or castle quickly enough.

F

Family Check A knight fork that attacks the opposing king, queen, and at least one rook. A triple fork. See ROYAL FORK or FAMILY FORK.

Family Fork Same as FAMILY CHECK and ROYAL FORK.

Fast Move A forcing move, usually a check, but also any capture or powerful threat that requires immediate response. See QUIET MOVE and SLOW MOVE.

Fegatello Attack The Italian name for the FRIED LIVER ATTACK of the Two Knights Defense, 1. e4 e5 2. Nf3 Nc6 3. Bc4 Nf6 4. Ng5 d5 5. exd5 Nxd5 6. Nxf7, a line of play popular with newcomers.

Feint A maneuver that seems to threaten one thing so as to gain time to carry out the real threat somewhere else. Usually it involves faking movement in one direction in order to move toward another. Similar to Reti's DIAGONAL MARCH.

W: Kd8 Pa4　(2)

B: Kb4 Pf6　(2)

QUESTION: How can White play and draw?

White cannot catch the Black pawn directly, for 1. Ke7 is met by 1. ... f5. The key is to gain time by first threatening to support the a-pawn.

ANSWER: After 1. Kc7! (seemingly moving away from the f-pawn) 1. ... f5 2. Kb6!!, Black must either capture the a-pawn, allowing his own to be overtaken, or continue 2. ... f4, when 3. a5 f3 4. a6 f2 5. a7 f1/Q 6. a8/Q ends in a drawn position.

Fianchetto A variation of the Italian word for "flank," used in chess to signify a bishop's development toward the flank (usually g2, g7, b2, or b7) rather than toward the center.

FIDE The abbreviation for the French Fédération Internationale des Échecs, the World Chess Federation, an international body that governs the play of the game. The USCF is America's representative in FIDE.

FIDE Laws of Chess See LAWS OF CHESS.

50-Move Rule One of the five ways to draw a chess game. A player may claim a draw if 50 moves have been played without a capture or a pawn move. The player must claim the draw just before making the 50th move, or any later move. If a capture or a pawn move is played during the interim, the count must start all over again. See DRAW.

File A vertical row of squares.

Finger-Fehler German for "finger slip." An obvious mistake or TOUCH-MOVE blunder.

Finesse A subtle tactic. Also, to play such a stratagem. See TACTICAL FINESSE.

Finite Capable of being determined, calculated, measured, or defined, as is chess itself according to game theory. Theoretically, if we could see far enough, every chess situation could be analyzed to its conclusion.

First Move White's first play, the move that starts the game. Loosely, it's also used to refer to Black's first move response.

First-Move Advantage The natural initiative that White has in starting the game.

First-Move Option   For each pawn's first move, the choice of moving one or two squares.

Fish   Slang for a weak player; one who thinks he's a lot better than he is and is therefore a prime target for chess gamblers and hustlers. See DUFFER, WOODPUSHER, and PATZER.

Fishcake   A weak player; a FISH.

Five-Minute Chess   A form of rapid transit chess in which each side has but five minutes to play the entire game. See RAPID TRANSIT and SPEED CHESS.

Fixed   Blocked or held in place, especially referring to mutually impeding white and black pawns.

Fixed Center   A center containing a pair of fixed pawns. The typical plan for such centers is to play to occupy your strongpoints—those squares guarded by your fixed center pawn.

Fixed Pawns   Two pawns—one white and one black—facing and blocking each other on the same file, so that neither can move.

Flag   A tab or pendulum at the top of a clock face that falls to indicate that time has expired. A chess clock has two faces, each with a flag.

Flank   Particularly the two outer rows on either side of the board; inclusively, the adjacent bishop files as well. See WING.

Flank Attack An assault on either flank, often with pawns to drive back enemy pieces that influence the center. In endgames, a rook attack along the rank.

Flanking a Bishop Developing a bishop in a FIANCHETTO.

Flank Opening An opening alignment in which the chief feature is a fianchettoed bishop. See HYPERMODERN OPENING and INDIAN SYSTEM.

Flight Square Any square to which the king can flee for safety. See ESCAPE SQUARE and LUFT.

Fool's Mate A quick mate with the queen along the K1-KR4 diagonal.

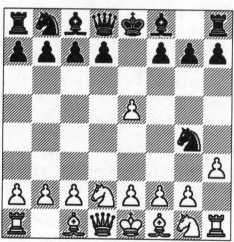

> W: Ke1 Qd1 Ra1 Rh1 Bc1 Bf1 Nd2 Ng1 Ps a2 b2 c2 e2 e5   (16)
> f2 g2 h3
> B: Ke8 Qd8 Ra8 Rh8 Bc8 Bf8 Nb8 Ng4 Ps a7 b7 c7 d7 f7   (15)
> g7 h7

QUESTION: How does Black win White's queen?

In a version of the shortest game possible, Black mates White in two moves: 1. f3 e5 2. g4 Qh4#. For White to mate Black comparably it takes three moves: 1. e4 g5 2. d4 f6 3. Qh5#.

ANSWER: The preceding moves were 1. d4 Nf6 2. Nd2 e5 3. dxe5 Ng4 4. h3. Now Black has the deadly intrusion 4. ... Ne3!, when 5. fxe3 runs into 5. ... Qh4+ 6. g3 Qxg3#, exploiting the e1-h4 diagonal. To avoid this mate, White must allow his queen to be captured.

Force Material. Also, to reduce the opponent to a single legal or practical move because the alternatives are unacceptable.

Forced Mate A mate that cannot be stopped if the attack is conducted correctly, no matter how accurate or resourceful the defense. See MATING NET.

Forcing Compelling the response, either because there are no other moves or because no other moves make sense.

Forcing Move A move for which the possible responses are limited and determinable. A forcing move leaves no legal or practical choice.

For Free Without giving up anything in exchange. It refers to capturing without being recaptured. See FOR NOTHING.

Forfeit To lose on time or by a penalty imposed by the TOURNAMENT DIRECTOR or ARBITER.

Fork An attack on at least two enemy units by a single unit with a single move. A form of DOUBLE ATTACK.

Forking Check A fork in which one of the attacked units is the king. A fork that's also a check.

W: Kf6 Bd3 Pg4   (3)
B: Kh6 Rd1   (2)

QUESTION: Can White eke out a draw?

The best forks are checks because they force the enemy to save the king, which may result in the abandonment of the other attacked enemy unit.

ANSWER: White does better than a draw with 1. g5+ Kh5 2. Be2+, a forking check mincing the rook.

Fork Trick A combination that wins a pawn or trades center pawns favorably. In a fork trick a piece (usually a knight) is temporarily sacrificed and then regained by a subsequent pawn fork. An example: 1. e4 e5 2. Nc3 Nf6 3. Bc4 Nxe4 4. Nxe4 d5.

For Nothing A phrase describing a one-sided exchange in which a player captures without being recaptured. See FOR FREE.

Fortress   In the endgame, a situation in which an inferior force, by setting up a defensive wall or barrier, can prevent a superior force from winning the game. See BISHOP OF THE WRONG COLOR and POSITIONAL DRAW.

W: Kh1 Qb4 Bg2 Nc3   (4)

B: Kh6 Qg3 Bd6   (3)

QUESTION: Can White to play save the game?

It's truly amazing how an impregnable defensive setup can sometimes be realized from skeletal forces. Here White's situation looks hopeless because it seems he must extricate his queen and also guard against mate at h2. Though it seems impossible, he can salvage a draw!

ANSWER: White draws by sacrificing the queen for the bishop, 1. Qxd6 + ! Qxd6 and following with 2. Ne4, and Black will be unable to penetrate White's fortress.

Forward   Toward the opponent's side. The only direction in which pawns can move.

Freeing Advance   A pawn move that unblocks a cramped position and releases one's pieces. Often an equalizing move or the start of meaningful counterplay.

Freeing Maneuver   A series of moves to exchange off a cumbersome piece or reposition it to improve mobility. The process may also enhance the scope of several other pieces.

Freeing Move   Either a pawn advance or piece exchange that gives breathing space to constricted forces.

Fried Liver Attack   See FEGATELLO ATTACK.

Friendly Forces   The pieces and pawns of one color; one side's collective material.

Friendly Game   An offhand game played for fun. See SKITTLES.

Front   The war zone; the area of direct confrontation, as determined by the placement of the pawns.

Frontal Attack   A direct attack by a rook on a passed pawn along the file in front of the pawn, as opposed to a rear attack from behind. Also, a blockading king attack in front of a pawn. See REAR ATTACK.

Frontier   An imaginary line dividing the board in half horizontally, separating the white side from the black. Also called FRONTIER LINE, the term was coined by Aron Nimzovich.

Frontier Line   See FRONTIER.

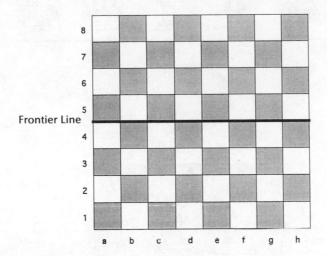

Front Rook When rooks are doubled on a file or rank, the first rook. The front rook is the one capable of capturing with backup from the other. See BACK ROOK.

Full Move A move by both White and Black. Either move separately is called a HALF-MOVE or a PLY.

Fundamentals The BASICS. Not just the moves and rules, but also the elementary principles of commendable play.

G

Gain a Move To establish the same position but with the other player to move. To complete an action, sequence, or plan in one less move than apparently needed or expected. To force the opponent to waste a move. Also called GAIN A TEMPO.

Gain a Tempo See GAIN A MOVE.

Gambit A voluntary sacrifice in the opening, usually of a pawn, offered to gain a positional advantage, build the initiative, or blunt the opponent's attack.

Gambiteer A specialist in opening gambits who enjoys playing them; often, a wild attacker.

Game of the Century

A game played between Donald Byrne and Bobby Fischer (Black) in New York in 1956 when Fischer was only thirteen years old.

W: Kf1 Qa3 Rd1 Rh1 Bc4 Bc5 Nf3 Ps a2 d4 f2 g2 h2   (12)

B: Kg8 Qb6 Ra8 Re8 Bg4 Bg7 Nc3 Ps a7 b7 c6 f7 g6 h7   (13)

QUESTION: What brilliant move does Black play?

The game was played in the Rosenwald Tournament held at the Marshall and Manhattan Chess Clubs. The appellation "game of the century" was coined by the theoretician Hans Kmoch, who, like most people, was enthralled by the genius of the young Fischer.

ANSWER: Fischer's extraordinary combination began with 1. ...Be6!!. Play continued 2. Bxb6 (2. Bxe6 loses to 2. ... Qb5+ 3. Kg1 Ne2+ 4. Kf1 Ng3+ 5. Kg1 Qf1+ 6. Rxf1 Ne2#) 2. ... Bxc4+ 3. Kg1 Ne2+ 4. Kf1 Nxd4+ 5. Kg1 Ne2+ 6. Kf1 Nc3+ 7. Kg1 axb6, and Bobby gets clear material and positional advantages. The game concluded 8. Qb4 Ra4 9. Qxb6 Nxd1 10. h3 Rxa2 11. Kh2 Nxf2 12. Re1 Rxe1 13. Qd8+ Bf8 14. Nxe1 Bd5 15. Nf3 Ne4 16. Qb8 b5 17. h4 h5 18. Ne5 Kg7 19. Kg1 Bc5+ 20. Kf1 Ng3+ 21. Ke1 Bb4+ 22. Kd1 Bb3+ 23. Kc1 Ne2+ 24. Kb1 Nc3+ 25. Kc1 Rc2#.

Game Theory A branch of mathematics that deals with decision-making in conflict situations.

General Principles Guidelines, maxims, rules of thumb, and practical advice. The same as PRINCIPLES.

Geometric Maneuver A series of moves that trace a pattern.

Give Odds To start a game with the handicap of less material, allowing the opponent extra moves or time, or accepting some other nonstandard limitation or stipulation.

GM The abbreviation for grandmaster. The official title conferred by FIDE is INTERNATIONAL GRANDMASTER.

Good Bishop A bishop that is unimpeded by its own pawns and is therefore well placed, with clear diagonals for attack. A good bishop is usually opposed by a BAD BISHOP.

Grande Combinaison A complex combination, blending different motifs, often profound, extending for five moves or more.

Grandmaster A loose reference to INTERNATIONAL GRANDMASTER, the highest title awarded by the World Chess Federation (FIDE).

Grandmaster Draw A lifeless draw in the opening of early middlegame. It's called a grandmaster draw because it seems to the unknowing public that grandmasters draw many of their games in this manner. (There may be reasons for such draws that amateurs fail to perceive, but sometimes they're right.)

Greco's Mate A standard mating attack initiated by a bishop sacrifice on h7 (or h2). Also called CLASSIC BISHOP SACRIFICE.

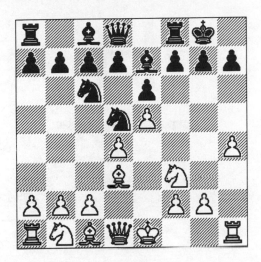

W: Ke1 Qd1 Ra1 Rh1 Bc1 Bd3 Nb1 Nf3 Ps a2 b2 c2 d4 e5   (16)
   f2 g2 h4

B: Kg8 Qd8 Ra8 Rf8 Bc8 Be7 Nc6 Nd5 Ps a7 b7 c7 d7 e6   (16)
   f7 g7 h7

QUESTION: How can White begin a winning attack?

Greco's sacrifice requires a bishop that can be sacrificed on h7 (or h2), and at least two, if not three or four, supporting units, especially the queen and the king-knight.

ANSWER: The winning attack goes 1. Bxh7+ Kxh7 2. Ng5+ Bxg5 (if 2. ... Kh8, then 3. Ng5) 3. hxg5+ Kg6 4. Qh5+ Kf5 5. Qh3+ Kg6 6. Qh7#.

Gueridon Mate A mating position that resembles a table, with the mate delivered by a queen and the two potential escape squares diagonally behind the mated king blocked by its own forces. It comes from the French term *gueridon,* meaning pedestal table, and is the same pattern as a SWALLOW'S-TAIL MATE.

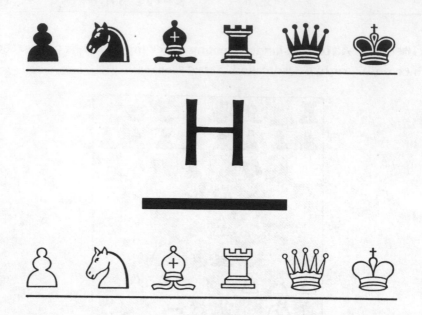

H

Half Move A move by White only or by Black only, which is one PLY. A FULL MOVE is a move for both White and Black, which is two PLY.

Half-Open File A file, occupied only by pawns of one color, that the opponent's major pieces can use for attack.

Half-Pin A position with two friendly pieces on the same line so that, if either moved off the line, the other would find itself in a pin.

Handicap Usually, a material disadvantage or a time differential at the start of a game offered to a weaker player to equalize the chances.

Hanging   Unprotected and exposed to capture. A related term is EN PRISE.

Hanging Pawns   Two adjacent friendly pawns occupying the same rank, usually subject to attack but sometimes capable of advancing with advantage.

Head Pawn   The most advanced in any formation. A term coined by Hans Kmoch (1894–1973) in his classic work *Pawn Power in Chess*.

Heavy Piece   A MAJOR PIECE; a queen or a rook.

Helpmate   A composed problem in which Black moves first and cooperates with White to get mated in a specified number of moves. Also, in ordinary chess talk, an epithet for a blunder leading to mate, especially if it's the only move allowing mate. See SELFMATE.

Heuristics   The art of problem solving. In chess, the use of a variety of techniques and methods, such as trial and error and posing probing questions, to test certain moves and variations, and to unearth useful information about the position.

Hold To survive an attack; to defend successfully.

W: Kc1 Bh3 Pd6   (3)
B: Kh4 Bc6 Ph2   (3)

QUESTION: Can White hold?

The diagram is from the end of a study by M. S. Liburkin. White seems to be in dire straits, but a clever rejoinder saves the day.

ANSWER: White holds by the spectacular 1. Bg2!!, when 1. ... Bxg2 2. d7 h1+ 3. Kd2 leads to the promotion of the d-pawn.

Holding-Off Maneuver In the endgame, an active defense by a king to prevent the approach of its counterpart.

Hole A weakness, usually a square on a player's third or fourth rank, that cannot be defended by a pawn and is therefore ideal for occupation by enemy pieces.

Home Analysis Opening analysis "cooked up" before playing a game, enabling one to achieve a certain desired position without much work at the board. See PREPARED ANALYSIS.

Horizontal Opposition   An opposition in which the kings line up on the same rank, separated by one, three, or five squares.

   Direct horizontal opposition has one square between, distant horizontal opposition three squares, and long-distant horizontal opposition five squares. See OPPOSITION.

Horizontal Row   A RANK. Starting from White's side of the board, the ranks are numbered from one to eight.

Horrwitz Bishops   See RAKING BISHOPS.

Hung   Left unprotected, as in "hung a pawn." See EN PRISE.

Hurdle   Another name for SKEWER.

Hypermodern   A school or style advocating several ideas opposed to classical principles, mainly to control the center initially from the flank rather than to occupy it directly. The term was first used by Savielly Tartakower (1887–1956) in the 1920s. See INDIAN.

Hypermodern Defense   A defense by Black that lets White set up a classical pawn center (pawns at d4 and e4) so that it can be undermined with off-center advances supported by a fianchettoed bishop. After gaining control of the center, the hypermodern defender hopes to occupy it with his own forces. See INDIAN DEFENSE.

Hypermodern Opening   See FLANK OPENING and INDIAN SYSTEM.

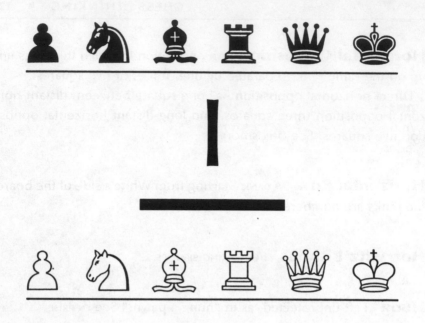

Ideal Mate A PURE MATE in which every unit on the board has a reason for being there. See MODEL MATE.

Illegal In violation of the moves and rules. See LEGAL.

Illegal Move A move that violates the rules of the game and therefore can't be played. See LEGAL MOVE. If an illegal move is played, it must be retracted.

Illegal Position A position not capable of occurring in a real chess game. Either the rules would have to have been broken or the situation is logically impossible. See LEGAL POSITION.

IM The abbreviation for INTERNATIONAL MASTER, a title conferred by FIDE.

Immortal Game An offhand game played between Anderssen (White) and Kieseritzky in London in 1851 in which Anderssen sacrificed his queen and two rooks.

W: Ke2 Qf3 Bd6 Nd5 Nf5 Ps a2 c2 d3 e5 g4 h5   (11)
B: Ke8 Qa1 Ra8 Rh8 Bc8 Bg1 Na6 Ng8 Ps a7 b5   (14)
    d7 f7 g7 h7

QUESTION: How does White mate in three moves?

The score of the game up to the diagram: 1. e4 e5 2. f4 exf4 3. Bc4 Qh4+ 4. Kf1 b5 5. Bxb5 Nf6 6. Nf3 Qh6 7. d3 Nh5 8. Nh4 Qg5 9. Nf5 c6 10. g4 Nf6 11. Rg1 cxb5 12. h4 Qg6 13. h5 Qg5 14. Qf3 Ng8 15. Bxf4 Qf6 16. Nc3 Bc5 17. Nd5 Qxb2 18. Bd6 Bxg1 19. e5 Qxa1+ 20. Ke2. Black resigned here, but considered playing 20. ... Na6 (the diagram).

ANSWER: Anderssen wins after 21. Nxg7+ Kd8 22. Qf6+!, with mate next move on e7.

Inaccuracy A slight error that makes it harder to achieve a win or hold a draw.

In-Between Move A move that interrupts an apparently forced sequence. A finesse that gains time or some other advantage. Also called ZWISCHENZUG.

Indian A term describing opening setups that run counter to traditional principles by relying on fianchettoed bishops, central pawn advances of only one square, off-center pawn thrusts, especially with the c-pawn, and initially allowing the opponent to establish a classical pawn center. The point of the Indian systems is to undermine this center and then take it over. See HYPERMODERN. The term also refers to any Indian system.

Indian Defense Any defense that answers 1. d4 with 1. ... Nf6. Often Black follows with a flank development on the kingside or queenside, trying to exert piece pressure against the white center. See INDIAN.

Indian System An opening setup for White or Black having the characteristics of an Indian defense. See INDIAN.

Indirect Not immediate or obvious, as in an INDIRECT THREAT.

Indirect Defense Defending a unit by preventing its capture tactically or practically instead of actually guarding it.

   An indirect defense might require a direct counterthreat, the removal or dislodging of the opponent's attacking unit, the setup of a clever concealed parry, or the exploitation of an already existing weakness that becomes vulnerable if the opponent routinely follows through with his own threat.

Indirect Threat A hidden attack, often prepared or set up by a direct one; the pretense of issuing one threat only to gain time for another.

Inductive Reasoning In chess, a method of formulating a strategy based on intuition and experience with similar situations by mentally trying out moves to determine their worth. What chessplayers do, for example, when they search for candidate moves. See DEDUCTIVE REASONING.

In Front Ahead of or before, especially applicable to pawns, as in stationing the king in front of a passed pawn.

W: Kb5 Pc4 (2)

B: Kd7 (1)

QUESTION: Should White advance the pawn?

As a rule, the king should try to clear a path in front of the passed pawn so that it can then advance with protection, convoyed to promotion.

ANSWER: White seizes a critical square, 1. Kb6, and the pawn cannot be stopped. A possible conclusion is 1. ... Kc8 2. Kc6 Kd8 3. Kb7 Kd7 4. c5, and the pawn goes in by force.

Initiative The ability to attack and force the play. An aspect of the element of TIME. The attacker has the initiative, the defender tries to blunt it and seize it.

Innovation A new move in an established opening, defense, or variation that often has theoretical value.

Innovative Creative, especially in the openings.

Insanity Chess A form of amateur tournament chess played under wild and difficult conditions, including ridiculously fast time controls, illogical pairings (such as playing the same player twice), and competing overnight.

Insufficient Mating Material One of the five ways to draw a chess game. A game is drawn if neither side has enough material to force mate. The term also refers to either side that is unable to force mate with what's left on the board.

In Tandem Cooperatively; said of two or more players playing as a team, but normally not consulting. See ALLIES.

Intangible Advantage Any positional (nonmaterial, nonstructural) superiority that could eventually dissipate unless converted into something concrete.

Interference The tactic of interposing a unit to cut an enemy piece's line of power, often with a time-gaining threat.

W: Kg1 Qd2 Rf1 Bg2 Ps a2 f2 g3 h2   (8)
B: Kg8 Qh5 Rf8 Na5 Ps a7 f6 g7 h7   (8)

QUESTION: How can White win a piece?

In most interferences the key is to block the line with a gain of time, particularly by giving a check. For the defender, getting out of check must take precedence over defending a piece.

ANSWER: White wins the knight by interfering with the Black queen's defense by a bishop check at d5. After 1. Bd5+ Kh8, White's queen can take the knight.

International Grandmaster   The highest title awarded by FIDE, the World Chess Federation.

International Master   The title just below INTERNATIONAL GRAND-MASTER, conferred by the World Chess Federation.

Interpose   To block an attack by moving a unit between the attacking piece and what it's attacking.

Interposition A block created to shield a friendly piece, especially the king.

W: Kd3 Ba2 Nc4 Pd4   (4)
B: Kd5 Rh3 Bc6 Pd6   (4)

QUESTION: How should White get out of check?

Not all interpositions are purely defensive. Some contain an element of counterattack and even a little poison.

ANSWER: Interposing the knight on e3, White gets out of check and incidentally discovers mate!

Intuitive Player Someone who moves by intelligent impulse rather than meticulous calculation. A natural, who has a good feel for positions; often a good speed player.

Irregular Opening A loose expression to characterize openings not beginning with double queen-pawn (1. d4 d5) or double king-pawn (1. e4 e5) moves. Not a very helpful classification.

Island Short for PAWN ISLAND.

Isolani   Nimzovich's term for the isolated queen-pawn, which can be a weakness or a strength, depending on circumstances. Often used to signify any isolated pawn.

Isolated D-Pawn   See ISOLATED QUEEN-PAWN.

Isolated Pawn   A pawn with no friendly pawns on adjacent files and therefore incapable of being defended by a pawn. Usually a weakness.

Isolated Pawn Pair   A weakness: two same-color, adjacent pawns, one protecting the other, neither of which can move because the opponent controls or occupies the squares immediately in front of them. The isolated pawn pair strives to become HANGING PAWNS, when although it may still be a weak complex it would have greater potential to advance.

Isolated Queen-Pawn   A special isolated pawn case. Usually it's an isolated white pawn at d4, though it could also refer to an isolated black pawn at d5.

In the opening and middlegame it tends to be an asset conferring a spatial edge (open files and more room behind the lines) while providing anchor for a centralized knight in the enemy half of the board. But in the endgame it's a disadvantage because it can't be protected by a pawn.

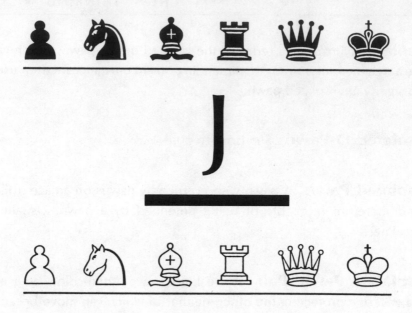

J'Adoube A French term that means "I adjust" or simply "adjust." Any of those terms are used to inform the opponent that you intend to straighten a piece, not move it. It's said immediately before touching the piece in question. See TOUCH-MOVE.

Jettison To abandon material to save the king or avoid loss of even greater material. Also, the name of the compulsory defensive tactic itself.

W: Kg1 Qg7 Re5 Ra1 Bc1 Bc4 Nb1 Ps a2 b2 d3 f2 g2 h3 (13)
B: Ke8 Qd8 Ra8 Rf8 Be7 Nc2 Nd5 Ps a7 b7 c6 f7 h7 (12)

QUESTION: How should White continue?

If your king needs immediate shelter or escape you may have to jettison a piece to survive. That was the case in the diagram, which stems from a game played by Danish superstar Bent Larsen (1935–).

ANSWER: White wins with 1. Rxd5!, when 1. ... cxd5 encounters 2. Bb5+, and Black is forced to jettison his queen on d7.

Judgment A general evaluation not necessarily based on concrete analysis but rather on experience with similar situations. See INDUCTIVE REASONING.

K

K The abbreviation for KING.

KB The abbreviation for KING-BISHOP.

KB-File The f-file; descriptive notation for KING-BISHOP FILE.

KBP The f-pawn; the abbreviation for KING-BISHOP PAWN in descriptive notation.

Keep Score To write the moves down.

Key The correct first move of the solution to a composed chess problem. If another move also works, the problem is said to have a COOK.

Key Opposition

The opposition between the two outer critical squares, leading to a TURNING MANEUVER. The opposition needed to achieve the goal, usually the occupation of a critical square. See OPPOSITION and CRITICAL SQUARES.

W: Kd2   (1)
B: Kc4 Pd5   (2)

QUESTION: What is Black's correct move?

The opposition is the tool used to fight for the critical squares. In the diagram the d5-pawn's critical squares are c3, d3, and e3. By taking the key opposition Black's king insures a winning turning maneuver.

ANSWER: Black plays 1. ... Kd4, seizing the critical opposition with the king between the two outer critical squares, c3 and e3. The game might continue: 2. Kc2 Ke3 3. Kd1 d4 4. Ke1 d3 5. Kd1 d2 6. Kc2 Ke2 and Black promotes next move.

Key Square

Another name for CRITICAL SQUARE.

Kibitz A Yiddish word that in chess means to make comments to the players during their game. A KIBITZER might do so after the game as well, when it's being analyzed.

Kibitzer A bystander who makes unsolicited comments on a game being played by others.

Kick To drive back an enemy piece, especially a minor piece, that has crossed the frontier line, by attacking it with a pawn.

As a rule of thumb, don't let enemy pieces stand in your half of the board. If you have the time, and the situation allows, drive them away, "kick" them out. See PUTTING THE QUESTION TO THE BISHOP.

Killer Instinct The desire to put the game away once you've achieved a winning position.

This is what Bobby Fischer supposedly has in abundance, and, according to him, either you have it or you don't. Some chessplayers are content to get a winning game, and then they let down their guard, thinking they've already won.

King The focus of the game of chess. Each side tries to checkmate the other side's king. The king moves one square in any direction but is not allowed to move into check. Abbreviated K.

King and Pawn Endgame See PAWN ENDING.

King-Bishop For either side, the bishop that starts the game on the kingside—f1 for White and f8 for Black.

King-Bishop File The f-file, as it is called in descriptive notation.

King-Bishop Pawn For either side, an f-pawn, as it is called in descriptive notation.

King File Descriptive notation for the e-file.

King Hunt A series of moves that chase a king around the board until it is mated or its owner is forced to surrender gobs of material. See MATING ATTACK.

  W: Ke1 Qh5 Ra1 Rh1 Bd3 Ne4 Ne5 Ps a2 b2 c2 d5 f2 g2 h2   (14)
  B: Kg8 Qe7 Ra8 Rf8 Bb7 Bf6 Nb8 Ps a7 b6 c7 d7 e6 g7 h7   (14)

QUESTION: Does White mate by taking on f6 with check?

The diagram comes from a famous game between Edward Lasker (White) and Sir George Thomas in London in 1912. After 1. Nxf6+, threatening to follow with a capture on h7, Black retakes with the g-pawn, suddenly allowing the queen to defend along its second rank.

ANSWER: Lasker's brilliant winning move was 1. Qxh7+!!. After 1. ... Kxh7 White let loose a ferocious king hunt: 2. Nxf6+ Kh6

3. Neg4+ Kg5 4. h4+ Kf4 5. g3+ Kf3 6. Be2+ Kg2 7. Rh2+ Kg1 8. Kd2#. Yes, 8. O-O-O is also mate.

King-Knight File   The descriptive name for the g-file.

King-Knight Pawn   The descriptive name for either side's g-pawn.

King March   A king maneuver, often along a critical diagonal, up and/or across the board.

King-Pawn   The descriptive name for either side's e-pawn.

King-Pawn Game   A game or opening beginning with the two-square advance of White's e-pawn, 1. e4.

King-Pawn Opening   See KING-PAWN GAME.

King-Rook File   The descriptive name for the h-file.

King-Rook Pawn   The descriptive name for either side's h-pawn.

King Safety   The degree to which a king is safe from attack, largely determined by the security of sheltering pawns. One of the five main elements of chess, along with TIME, SPACE, PAWN STRUCTURE, and MATERIAL.

King's Field All the squares adjacent to the king. Used as a term in tactics to describe general attacks to the king and the surrounding area.

W: Kb1 Qe5 Ba1 Nd4 Ps a2 b3 g2 h5   (8)

B: Kg8 Qc7 Rc8 Rf8 Ps f7 g7 h7   (7)

QUESTION: How can White mate in three moves?

Black's king looks all nice and cozy behind the cover of three king-side pawns, but now it's White's move.

ANSWER: It's mate after detonating the king's field: 1. Qxg7+!! Kxg7 2. Nf5+ Kg8 3. Nh6#.

Kingside The half of the board occupied by the kings at the start, consisting of the e-, f-, g-, and h-files. It is called the kingside even if the kings eventually wind up on the QUEENSIDE.

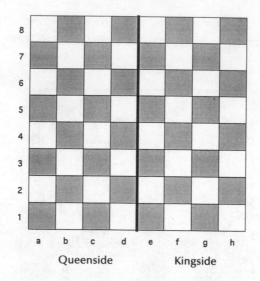

Queenside   Kingside

Kingside Attack   A general attack of a number of units aimed at the enemy king's position, usually after it's castled kingside.

Kingside Castling   Castling with the king-rook, toward the h-file. The move is written "O-O." See CASTLING.

King's Wing   The kingside, usually not counting the e-file.

KN   The descriptive abbreviation for KING-KNIGHT.

KN-File   The descriptive abbreviation for KING-KNIGHT FILE.

Knight   One of the six different types of chess units. The move of the knight resembles a capital L.

Each side starts the game with two knights. White's begin on b1 and g1, Black's on b8 and g8. It's symbolized N to avoid confusion with the symbol for king, K.

Knight Corral A bishop trap of a knight on the edge. See CORRAL.

Knight Ending An ending with knights and pawns.

Knight Fork Any double attack by a knight. See FAMILY FORK and ROYAL FORK.

W: Kb4 Nd3 Pg2   (3)
B: Ka6 Qf6 Pa7   (3)

QUESTION: Can White to move survive?

You can't expect knight forks to be served to you on a plate. Often you have to set them up.

ANSWER: White survives and then some with 1. Nc5+ Kb6 2. Nd7+, a devastating knight fork.

Knight Odds A typical handicap, in which the odds giver (usually White) starts the game without the queen-knight.

Knight on the Rim Is Dim A maxim advising against moving knights to the edge, where their mobility is reduced (though it's often necessary to move them to the outer files). Sometimes given as "a knight on the rim is grim."

Knights Before Bishops An opening maxim suggesting that the best way to develop the minor pieces is to bring out at least one knight before developing a bishop. While the concept seems to apply to many situations, it's actually a very inexact principle that should not be applied rigidly.

Knight's Jump Away An expression signifying the length and shape of a knight's move. A unit that's a knight's jump away from a knight is in position to be captured by the knight if circumstances permit. Also described as "knight's move away."

Knight's Move Opposition An opposition in which the kings are separated by the distance of a knight's move. It applies in situations where standard straight-line oppositions are not available because fixed pawns block and guard typical oppositional squares. See TRÉBU-CHET and THEORY OF CORRESPONDING SQUARES.

Knight's Tour A puzzle or task in which a knight is to be moved over an otherwise empty board, visiting each square only once.

KN-Pawn The descriptive name for either side's g-pawn.

KP The descriptive abbreviation for KING-PAWN. Especially useful for opening discussions.

KR The descriptive abbreviation for KING-ROOK.

Kriegspiel A form of chess in which players sit at separate boards and play standard chess without seeing their opponent's moves. The actual moves by both sides are made on a master board by the arbiter, who says only whether or not a move is legal. There is no penalty for playing an illegal move. In fact, deliberately illegal moves are how the players learn the locations of enemy pieces.

KRP The descriptive abbreviation for KING-ROOK PAWN.

Lateral Thinking The creative use of knowledge and insight in one area to solve a problem in another; nonlinear reasoning; shifting perspective to get a fresh viewpoint. Chessplayers do this with facility. Also called DIVERGENT THINKING. See ANALOGUE and CRITICAL THINKING.

Laws of Chess The MOVES AND RULES as officially sanctioned and applied by FIDE, the World Chess Federation. Rules for tournament competition in the United States are defined by its affiliate, the USCF. Also called FIDE LAWS OF CHESS.

Legal A permissible move or a position reached via legal moves. A legal move may be played; an illegal move may not. A *legal position* may be achieved in a real chess game; an ILLEGAL POSITION may not.

Legal Move A move allowed by the LAWS OF CHESS.

Legal's Mate A mate with two or three minor pieces against an uncastled king stemming from an unpinning combination, discovered by a famous 18th-century player named Legal. See LEGAL'S SACRIFICE.

An example of Legal's mate occurs in the following game: 1. e4 e5 2. Nf3 d6 3. Bc4 Bg4 4. Nc3 g6? 5. Nxe5! Bxd1 6. Bxf7+ Ke7 7. Nd5#.

Legal's Sacrifice An unpinning combination. It either entails the sacrifice of a piece (usually a bishop) with a SETUP CHECK to be followed by an unpinning check that regains the piece (usually the opponent's pinning bishop), or simply unpins, offering the queen with a sting: take the queen and fall into Legal's mate.

W: Kg1 Qd1 Ra1 Bg5 Nf1 Ps d5 e4 f2 g2   (9)

B: Kg7 Qe7 Rh8 Bb6 Nf6 Ps c7 d6 e5 g6   (9)

QUESTION: What should Black do about the pin on his knight?

Newcomers often stumble into Legal's sacrifice by developing the queen-bishop prematurely to pin the opponent's king-knight. Not all pins are great.

ANSWER: Black should unleash an unpinning combination, continuing 1. ... Bxf2+! 2. Kxf2 Nxe4+, regaining the sacrificed bishop with a powerful attack. Black also wins by 1. ... Nxe4!

Lever A pawn attack at the base of an opponent's pawn chain. More often, any pawn advance leading to BREAKTHROUGH pawn exchanges.

Lightning Chess Speed chess. See RAPID TRANSIT CHESS.

Light on the Right Rule The rule determining the board's correct placement at the game's start: with a light square in the near corner at each player's right.

Light Pieces Bishops and knights. Also called MINOR PIECES. Sometimes, inexactly, the white pieces.

Light-Square Bishop A bishop that travels only on light squares. For White, the bishop starting on f1; for Black, the bishop starting on c8.

Light-Square Game A game in which the most desirable plan seems to be to control, occupy, and influence the central light squares, especially involving a fianchettoed light-square bishop. See DARK-SQUARE GAME.

Light-Square Rule See LIGHT ON THE RIGHT RULE.

Line Any number of consecutive squares along a rank, file, or diagonal.

Linear Thinking Reasoning one-dimensionally with strict adherence to sequence and the attainment of a definite goal. What chessplayers do, for example, when solving a posed tactical problem with known consequences. See LATERAL THINKING.

Line-Piece Any piece capable of moving along a line of squares; a queen, a rook, or a bishop.

Liquidate To exchange, especially in the sense of ridding oneself of a weakness or problem.

Liquidation Exchanging to reduce the intensity of your opponent's attack and/or simplify to a superior, manageable endgame. The policy of trading to establish clarity.

W: Kh1 Rb2 Pa4   (3)
B: Kh6 Rg4   (2)

QUESTION: Should White push the pawn or protect it?

Instead of protecting an attacked unit, get rid of the attacker and there may be no need to protect.

ANSWER: The best continuation is 1. Rh2 + ! Kg5 2. Rg2, pinning Black's rook and forcing a trade, after which the pawn goes in to queen uncontested.

Little Center A position in which a pair of central pawns have been traded so that one side has a pawn on its fourth rank vs. an opposing pawn on its third rank.

An example is a white pawn at e4 vs. a Black pawn at d6. Whoever has the more advanced pawn (White here) retains a spatial edge and perhaps the better chances, while the side with the less advanced pawn (Black) is considered to have the little center.

Live Side In pawn endings, the side of the board closest to the PROTECTED PASSED PAWN or attacking zone. The BLIND SIDE tends to be the more distant area, away from the immediate fight.

Living Chess An exhibition chess game between two players or teams, usually played on a field or in a very large room, in which people dressed in costumes portray the pieces and move as directed by the players.

Long Diagonal Either of the two longest diagonals: a1-h8 or a8-h1. Loosely, the longest of any two intersecting diagonals.

Long-Distant Diagonal Opposition See LONG-DISTANT OPPOSITION.

Long-Distant Horizontal Opposition See LONG-DISTANT OPPOSITION.

Long-Distant Opposition An opposition along a file, rank, or diagonal in which the kings are separated by five squares. LONG-DISTANT VERTICAL OPPOSITION is along a file, LONG-DISTANT HORIZONTAL OPPOSITION is along a rank, and LONG-DISTANT DIAGONAL OPPOSITION is along a diagonal. See OPPOSITION.

Long-Distant Vertical Opposition
A long-distant opposition along a file.

W: Kg2 Ps c4 d5   (3)
B: Kf8 Pd6   (2)

QUESTION: How does White play and win?

It may seem that White should simply charge up the board and advance the c-pawn, effecting an exchange that produces a passed d-pawn. But that doesn't work because the black king can eventually get a meaningful opposition.

ANSWER: White wins by taking the long-distant vertical opposition with 1. Kf2!. After 1. ... Ke7 2. Kg3 Kf7 3. Kf3 White has the distant opposition. And after 3. ... Ke7 4. Kg4 Kf6 5. Kf4 White has the direct opposition, which is transferred further up the board after 5. ... Ke7 6. Kg5 Kf7 7. Kf5. Black must then give way and allow White to outflank him: 7. ... Ke7 8. Kg6 Ke8 9. Kf6 Kd7 10. Kf7, forcing the gain of the d-pawn.

Long-Range Piece
Any line-piece; a queen, a rook, or a bishop.

Long Side The side of the board with the greater number of files from a pawn to the edge of the board. See SHORT SIDE.

The concept is particularly important in rook endgames in which the rook must be far enough from the opposing king to give a successful flank attack. Thus the suggestion "move your rook to the long side." See CHECKING DISTANCE.

Lose To get checkmated, resign, forfeit on time, or be disqualified for violating the rules. In chess competition, a player gets nothing for a loss and one point for a win. Each player gets half a point on a DRAW.

Lose a Move To create ZUGZWANG by making it your opponent's turn to move, especially at an undesirable moment.

Lose on Time To forfeit a game by failing to complete a specified number of moves in the allotted time. This is a factor in tournament play, where clocks are used to keep track of each player's time.

Losing the Exchange Losing a rook for a minor piece. See EXCHANGE.

Lost Said of a position that should lose if the opponent plays correctly. Also, said of the player with such a position, as in "you're lost."

Lost the Right to Castle A phrase meaning that the king has already moved and can no longer castle. The right to castle is also lost on either side by moving the rook on that side.

Lucena's Position In endings, a technique to create shelter from rook checks. Wrongly attributed to Luis Ramirez Lucena (15th–16th century), it was first published by Alessandro Salvio (1575–1640).

W: Kf2 Rb8   (2)

B: Kc1 Re6 Pc2   (3)

QUESTION: How does Black find shelter for his king?

The technique is also known as "building a bridge," which is how Nimzovich referred to it. It involves lifting the attacking rook to the fourth rank, where it can be used to interpose against enemy rook checks. See BRIDGE and BUILDING A BRIDGE.

ANSWER: Black wins after 1. Re5 Rb7 2. Kd2 Rd7+ 3. Kc3 Kc8+ 4. Kd3 Rd8+ 5. Kc4 Rc8+ 6. Rc4—end of story.

Luft   A German term meaning "air" or, figuratively, breathing space. An escape square for the king. When you move a pawn to create an escape square in front of your castled king you "make luft." A way to avoid back-rank mates.

Lust to Expand   A colorful expression with which Nimzovich characterized the value of a passed pawn: its need to advance toward promotion.

M

Main Line The primary variation, especially in an opening.

Majority Over any consecutive set of files, a group of pawns that outnumber their enemy counterparts. See PAWN MAJORITY.

Major Piece A queen or rook. Also called a HEAVY PIECE.

Make Luft In a castled position, to create an escape hatch for the king by moving a pawn. See LUFT.

Man Any of the 32 chess units that constitute a chess set. A shortened version of the sexist term "chessman."

Maneuver The repositioning of a piece, usually over the course of several moves. Also, to transfer a piece mainly with QUIET MOVES to a superior square.

W: Kh1 Ra1 Ne7 Ps a4 b3 c2 d3 e2 f4 f6 g2   (11)
B: Kh8 Ps a5 b4 c3 d4 e3 f7 g4 g3   (9)

QUESTION: How can White mate in eight moves?

Of course White can win the above position by bringing the knight back to win a few pawns, but checkmate is so much more final.

ANSWER: It's simple. Maneuver the white king to a2 (that takes seven moves) and then use an eighth move to mate with the rook at h1.

Maróczy Bind A type of pawn position in which white pawns at c4 and e4 (no d-pawn) restrain Black's pawns at d6 and e7. The term also applies to a comparable setup with colors reversed. Named after the Hungarian grandmaster Géza Maróczy (1870–1951).

Master An unofficial title for a strong player, not necessarily with ELO RATING of 2200 or more. See NATIONAL MASTER.

Match A set of games between the same two players or teams, as opposed to tournaments, in which each competitor plays different players.

Mate The end of the game. Short for CHECKMATE.

Material Pieces and pawns collectively or individually.

Material Advantage Having more material and a greater point count using the relative exchange values. See MATERIAL SUPERIORITY.

Material Superiority The same as MATERIAL ADVANTAGE. Usually a decisive factor.

Mating Attack A general assault against the king that leads to mate or significant gain of material.

Mating Material Enough material to force checkmate. A typical minimum mating force is a rook, though an extra pawn may be sufficient because it can be promoted.

Mating Net A position in which mate is forced.

W: Kg1 Ra7 Bh1 Ne5 Pg2   (5)
B: Kf8 Rh2 Ba8 Ne8 Ph7   (5)

QUESTION: Should White's rook take the bishop?

A distinction is made between mating attacks and mating nets. In a mating attack mate isn't forced because the defender can abandon material to postpone defeat. But no defense can stave off a mating net.

ANSWER: Why take the bishop when you can force mate? White does so by 1. Rf7+ Kg8 2. Bxh7+ Kh8 3. Ng6#.

Meaningful Opposition In certain endgames, the opposition that enables either the attacker to achieve a winning entry or the defender to bar the door to the invasion. Not every OPPOSITION is desirable or meaningful.

Men The 32 pieces and pawns considered collectively.

Methodical In chess, executing a plan in a careful, deliberate manner; systematic.

Middlegame The second phase of a chess game, after the opening and before the endgame, characterized by planning and maneuvering, and by trying to achieve a smooth transition to the endgame.

Miniature A short chess game that features nice tactical points. Also, a composed problem with no more than seven units on the board (including the kings). See BRILLIANCY and BREVITY.

W: Ka8 Qe6 Ne8 Ps a7 b7   (5)
B: Kf8 Pe7   (2)

QUESTION: How can White mate in two moves?

It was once thought that composed problems have little practical value because the positions tend to be materially one-sided. Furthermore, the astonishing solutions never seem to occur over the board. Teachers are now reconsidering the issue, reasoning that the atypical situations posed by problems and especially studies can stimulate the student's creativity.

ANSWER: White wins with the underpromotion 1. b8/N!. After 1. ... Kxe8 the problem concludes with 2. Qg8#.

Mining Operation A pawn advance to engage enemy pawns, leading to a trade and the opening of a file. A term used by Nimzovich.

Minor Exchange A term signifying the slight material edge a bishop has over a knight. You win the minor exchange if you gain a bishop for a knight.

Minority Attack An assault by several pawns against a larger group of pawns, attempting to inflict weaknesses that can then be attacked by pieces.

Minor Pieces Bishops and knights.

Mobile Center The same as MOBILE PAWN CENTER.

Mobile Pawn Center A center with two connected pawns, usually aligned on their fourth rank, opposed by a single enemy pawn, usually on its third rank, when the united pawns have the possibility of advancing.

Mobility Freedom of movement. The number of squares and/or options available to a piece. An aspect of SPACE.

Model Mate   A problem composition term: a pure mate in which there are no extraneous or superfluous units or functions and in which all of the attacker's units (in some cases excepting the king and pawns) are required. See CLEAN MATE, PURE MATE, and IDEAL MATE.

W: Ka1 Qh1 Rg1 Bb4   (4)
B: Kc2 Bd1   (2)

QUESTION: How does White mate in two moves?

This is a version of a problem published by P. H. Williams in 1897. Its art seems removed from actual game positions, since Black probably would have resigned a long time ago.

ANSWER: The key is 1. Rg4. If 1. ... bishop moves, then 2. Qb1#; if 1. ... Kc1, then 2. Rc4#; if 1. ... Kb3, then 2. Qxd1#; and if 1. ... Kd3, then 2. Qe4#.

Monster Chess A teaching technique, developed by Bruce Alberston, in which students practice making captures in sequence, leading to the removal of the enemy king. Monster pawn illustrates the use of the pawn; Monster bishop shows how to capture with a bishop; Monster rook with a rook, etc.

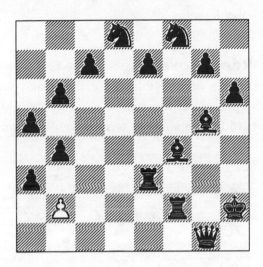

W: Pb2   (1)

B: Kh2 Qg1 Re3 Rf2 Bg5 Bf4 Ps g7 h6 Nd8 f8 Ps a3 h4 a5 b6   (16)
   c7 e7

QUESTION: What is the right sequence for capturing everything?

Don't apply the rules of standard chess in attempting to solve this problem. In Monster chess pawns may capture backward and may move to the back rank and then return the other way, and the king is allowed to stay in check. Moreover, White's king can be absent.

ANSWER: Starting from b2 the pawn goes to a3 to b4 to a5 to b6 to c7 to d8 to e7 to f8 to g7 to h6 to g5 to f4 to e3 to f2 to g1 to h2.

Move A turn for either side, or a turn for both sides. A turn for one side is more precisely called a HALF MOVE and a turn for both sides a FULL MOVE. Also, to make a move. See PLY.

Move on Move A form of speed chess in which each player responds to the opponent's move instantly. The games can be quite exciting.

Moves and Rules The laws of the game; how to play the game, but not how to play it well.

Mysterious Rook Move A rook move to a closed file or rank, which seems to make no sense because the rook's line of attack is blocked. But the player has foreseen a possibility for attack or deterrence and wants to be prepared. A term coined by Nimzovich.

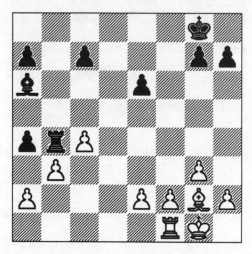

W: Kg1 Rf1 Bg2 Ps a2 b3 c4 e2 f2 g3 h2   (10)
B: Kg8 Rb4 Ba6 Ps a4 a7 c7 e6 g7 h7   (9)

QUESTION: How can White defend his queenside pawns?

The above position comes from the game Vaganyan–Nogueiras, Montpelier 1985. If White plays 1. Rb1 Black can counter 1. ... Bxc4 because White's b-pawn is pinned; and 1. bxa4 leaves all the queenside pawns vulnerable.

ANSWER: White holds with the mysterious rook move, 1. Ra1!, when 1. ... axb3 2. axb3 suddenly opens the a-file for rook counterplay. Vaganyan eventually won after 2. ... Bb7 3. Bxb7 Rxb7 4. Kf1 a5 5. Ke1 Kf7 6. Kd2 axb3 7. axb3 Rxb3 8. Rxa5 Rb2+ 9. Kd3 Ke7 10. h4 Rb3+ 11. Kc2 Bb7 12. f3 Kd6 13. h5 h6 14. Ra8 c6 15. Kc3 Rf7 16. Kd4 e5+ 17. Ke4 Re7 18. Ra5 Re7 19. Rxe5 (1-0).

N Abbreviation for KNIGHT.

National Master Usually the highest title awarded by a national chess organization. See INTERNATIONAL MASTER.

NN An abbreviation that indicates a player whose name is not known, sometimes used in the score of an exhibition game against an amateur.

Noah's Ark Trap   In the Ruy Lopez (1. e4 e5 2. Nf3 Nc6 3. Bb5) a famous trap of the White king-bishop by Black's queenside pawns.

W: Kg1 Qd4 Ra1 Rf1 Bb3 Bc1 Nb1 Ps a2 b2 c2 e4 f2 g2 h2   (14)

B: Ke8 Qd8 Ra8 Rh8 Bc8 Be7 Nf6 Ps a6 b5 c7 d6 f7 g7 h7   (14)

QUESTION: How can Black play and win a piece?

Starting from the Ruy Lopez the diagram is reached after 3. ... a6 4. Ba4 Nf6 5. O-O d6 6. d4 b5 7. Bb3 exd4 8. Nxd4 Nxd4 9. Qxd4. Actually, similar traps can occur in other openings, but the most familiar develops in this opening.

ANSWER: Black wins a piece with 9. ... c5, and when White retreats the queen, then 10. ... c4, snaring the bishop.

Notation   Any method for recording the moves of a chess game.

NP   The descriptive abbreviation for knight-pawn, which has particular utility in the classification of certain endings.

Objective Basing moves, evaluations, and decisions on the actual facts and circumstances and not on personal considerations or for arbitrary reasons. See SUBJECTIVE.

Oblique Opposition Another name for RECTANGULAR OPPOSITION.

Obstruct To force an enemy unit to a particular square so that no other enemy unit can use the square or pass across it.

Obstruction A piece or pawn that blocks the movement of another piece. Also, the name of the tactic.

Occupation Direct placement of a piece or pawn on a specific square. Also, absolute control of a file.

Odds See HANDICAP.

Offhand Games Games played without tournament conditions. Friendly, casual games played for fun. See SKITTLES.

One-Mover A problem that can be solved in one move. Also, a direct threat with an obvious point, as in a "one-move threat."

W: Kg1 Qf8 Ra4 (3)

B: Kg3 (1)

QUESTION: How can White mate in one move?

Some one-movers are so unexpected that they escape our notice. But they're there, waiting to be missed.

ANSWER: It's all over after 1. Qa3#.

Open Board A board with few or no obstructing pawns, allowing pieces to traverse it easily.

Open Center A center unblocked by pawns.

Open centers are conducive to sudden attacks, so development and king safety are important. After castling, it's usually unwise to move the pawns in front of the king, because the unblocked center offers possibilities for fast mating attacks.

Open File A file devoid of pawns. Sometimes a half-open file is described as "open" for the player able to use it.

Open Game A game or opening in which at least a pair of center pawns have been exchanged, so that movement through the center is possible. Open games naturally develop from the beginning moves 1. e4 e5. Also called OPEN POSITION.

Opening The beginning phase of a chess game, usually lasting 10 or 15 moves, sometimes longer. Development, control of the center, king safety, and the fight for the initiative are its paramount concerns.

Opening Line A variation in any opening.

Opening a File Generally, clearing a file for your own use by exchanging away a pawn blocking it. An action particularly helpful to rooks.

Opening Repertoire The set of opening lines for White and Black that a player regularly uses.

Openings The moves by both sides at the beginning of a game that have been analyzed and played so often that they have become standard.

Open Line A rank, file, or diagonal unobstructed by pawns.

Open Position The type of position likely to arise from an OPEN GAME.

Open Tournament A tournament open to players of any strength who are members of the governing chess federation.

Opposite-Color Bishops Also called *Opposite-Colored Bishops*. See BISHOPS OF OPPOSITE COLORS.

Opposition In endgames, a ZUGZWANG relationship between opposing kings that confers an advantage on the player not on the move.

If the kings "stand in opposition," whichever moves is at a disadvantage because it must give ground. The kings use the opposition in their fight to control a passed pawn's CRITICAL SQUARES The attacking king "takes the opposition," trying to occupy a critical square, and the defending king tries to "keep the opposition" to prevent the enemy king from occupying that critical square or others. In standard oppositions (vertical, horizontal, or diagonal; and direct, distant, and long-distant), the kings occupy squares of the same color separated by one, three, or five squares along the same file, rank, or diagonal. See DIRECT OPPOSITION, DISTANT OPPOSITION, DIAGONAL OPPOSITION, and RECTANGULAR OPPOSITION.

Oppositional Field The interrelation of every possible opposition, taken in series, extending across the entire board. Thus, a player with the long-distant opposition can convert it to a distant opposition as the opponent's king approaches, and then to a direct opposition if the king steps even closer. See OPPOSITION.

Original Position The initial placement of the board and arrangement of forces at the beginning of a game. See ARRAY.

Outflanking In endgames with fixed pawns, a flank invasion by one king against the other, usually to gain material.

W: Ke5 Pg5 (2)
B: Kf7 Pg6 (2)

QUESTION: How can White force a win?

A king can win a lone fixed pawn by occupying any of the three CRITICAL SQUARES to the right or left of the target pawn on the same rank. In the diagram, White's king can force the win of Black's g-pawn by occupying f6, e6, or d6.

ANSWER: White outflanks, wins the g-pawn, and then promotes. A possible variation: 1. Kd6 (occupying a critical square) Kf8 2. Ke6 Kg7 3. Ke7 Kg8 4. Kf6 Kh7 5. Kf7 Kh8 6. Kxg6 Kg8 7. Kh6 Kh8 8. g6 Kg8 9. g7 Kf7 10. Kh7 and the pawn soon queens.

Outpost A weak square, usually on the opponent's third or fourth rank, that the opponent can't guard with a pawn. Such a square, supported by at least one friendly pawn, can be occupied by a piece to good effect. From the defender's point of view, such a square is a HOLE.

Outside Critical Square In any set of three critical squares, the one farthest from the enemy king. See UNDERPASS and CROSSOVER.

Overextension The advance of pawns or pieces so far that they can't be properly supported. An overextended position is vulnerable to counterattack.

Overload   A tactic exploiting an overburdened piece's inability to fulfill all its defensive commitments.

W: Ke1 Qd1 Bb3 Pe3   (4)
B: Ke8 Qd8 Bc6 Ps e7 f7   (5)

QUESTION: Should White trade queens and then win the f-pawn?

When you have a possible two-move sequence, consider what would happen if you made the second move first.

ANSWER: Play the second move first here, 1. Bxf7 + !, and White wins the black queen by deflecting the king.

Overpass   A king maneuver across the path of a passed pawn to reach the OUTSIDE CRITICAL SQUARE. See CROSSOVER.

Overprotection   Guarding a key square with more pieces than necessary so that, if an exchange takes place there, a piece can take back instead of a pawn. Thus the square can still be used. Also, adding protection to relieve other defending units or to be ready for any contingency. The concept was deeply analyzed by Nimzovich.

Over the Board   Actual competition, as opposed to study or theory. An idea may work beautifully in home analysis, but against a real opponent anything can happen.

Overworked Piece   An OVERLOADED piece that can't fulfill all its protective commitments.

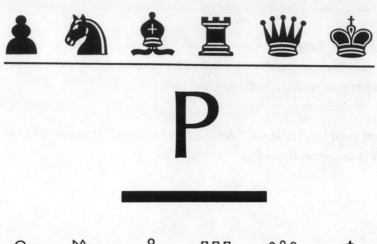

P

P The abbreviation for pawn, though in recording algebraic chess moves the symbol is not used.

Pairing The process of assigning opponents and colors in tournaments. Also, any particular matchup.

Pairing Charts See PAIRING TABLES.

Pairing Tables Charts for ROUND-ROBIN TOURNAMENTS indicating the round, the opponents, and their colors.

ROUND	PAIRINGS	
1	1:4	2:3
2	4:3	1:2
3	2:4	3:1

In round 1 of the above four-player round-robin the chart indicates that player 1 has White against player 4, while player 2 has White against player 3.

Parallel Architecture The ability of some computer programs to approach the solution of problems in two different ways simultaneously: by brute force calculation and by relying on complex algorithms for sophisticated generalizations.

Parry a Check To end a check by interposing a friendly unit.

Passed Pawn A pawn capable of advancing to promotion because no enemy pawns can block it or guard squares in its path. It has "passed" the opposition's pawns.

Passed Pawns Must Be Pushed A maxim exhorting the player to advance a passed pawn so that it becomes a threat to queen. The point is threefold: either to make a new queen, or to force the opponent to concede material, or simply to divert enemy resources.

Passive Defensive or inactive; designed merely to guard, ward off threats, or mark time, in contradistinction to an aggressive attack or counterattack. See ACTIVE.

Passive Rook In certain endings, a rook that merely protects against mate or is tied to defense.

W: Kd6 Rh7 Pe6   (3)
B: Kd8 Rg8   (2)

QUESTION: Can White to move eke out a win?

An active rook is one that can position itself for counterplay either from behind a passed pawn or from the flank. A passive rook, on the other hand, lacks counterattacking punch.

ANSWER: White wins at once with 1. Ra7, shifting to the other flank and menacing a check at a8. Black gets mated or skewered.

Pattern Recognition Discerning relationships or visual similarities between positions or situations and using them to formulate plans and solve problems. See ANALOGUE and CRITICAL THINKING.

Patzer A weak player. From the German, meaning bungler. See ANT, BEGINNER, DUFFER, FISH, FISHCAKE, WOODPUSHER, and RABBIT.

Pawn One of the six different types of units, the pawn is the least valuable, worth only one point. Its abbreviation is P.

Pawn and Move A handicap in which, to begin a game, the stronger player removes a pawn (usually the f-pawn) and also accepts the black pieces, giving his opponent the first move. Also a way to describe a weak player's abilities: "He's pawn and move."

Pawn and Two Moves A handicap in which a player accepts the black pieces, removes his f pawn, and allows White two moves to begin the game. This is virtually a forced win for White—unless White is a very weak player.

Pawn Center A distinctive arrangement of center pawns that determines the game's character.

If the center is clear of pawns, tactics and quick attacks reign. If the center is impeded by interlocked pawns of both colors, play tends to proceed gradually, with both sides having more time for maneuvering.

Pawn Chain An interlocking group of friendly and enemy pawns blocking each other's movement. White's pawns form one obstructive diagonal (or chain), Black's another. Loosely, any diagonal series of same-color pawns. See FIXED PAWNS and ATTACK AT THE BASE OF THE PAWN CHAIN.

Pawn Configuration See PAWN FORMATION.

Pawn Duo Two aligned pawns on adjacent files, each possessing the ability to support the other's advance. See CONNECTED PAWNS.

Pawn Ending An endgame with just kings and pawns. Also called KING AND PAWN ENDGAME.

Pawn Fork A simultaneous attack by one pawn against two enemy units. See FORK TRICK.

W: Kf4 Rd1 Ps e4 g3 (4)
B: Kf6 Rb6 Bd6 (3)

QUESTION: Where should White move his king?

The more subtle forks need to be prepared. Inexperienced players often become frustrated because they look for obvious one-move forks that are easily averted, instead of trying to set them up in two or three moves. You can learn to disguise your intentions by practicing looking ahead.

ANSWER: The trick is the setup sacrifice 1. Rxd6 + !. After 1. ... Rxd6 2. e5 + , White simplifies to a won pawn ending.

Pawn Formation   The overall arrangement of pawns or any specific group of pawns. Also called PAWN CONFIGURATION. See PAWN STRUCTURE.

Pawn Game   A simpler version of chess used as a teaching tool in the original Manhattan Chess Club School and related programs. Students play only with kings and pawns initially, capturing and trying to win pawn races. Eventually they add the other pieces, piece by piece, as the situation warrants. This allows them to play right from the start, before they've learned all the moves and rules.

Pawn-Grabber   Someone who captures pawns that may not be safe to capture. Also called PAWN SNATCHER.

Pawn-Grabbing   The hazard of taking pawns at the expense of development and position. See POISONED PAWN.

Pawn Island   A pawn or group of pawns separated from other friendly pawns by at least one file. Usually, the fewer the islands, the easier it is to defend the pawns. Also referred to as an ISLAND.

Pawn Majority   A troop of friendly pawns outnumbering enemy pawns over the same number of files.

A player with a healthy pawn majority can create a passed pawn. When both sides castle kingside, a player with a queenside majority can produce a passed pawn and use it as a decoy to lure the enemy king from the kingside, possibly leaving that sector defenseless. See QUEENSIDE MAJORITY and CAPABLANCA'S RULE.

Pawn Promotion   See PROMOTION.

Pawn Race An actual race between black and white pawns to see which can promote first.

W: Kc7 Pa2   (2)
B: Kh6 Pg7   (2)

QUESTION: White to play. Is the game drawn?

In most pawn races promoting first is cardinal. The first side to get a new queen is usually the first to give check, before the other side has time to organize a defense.

ANSWER: By winning the pawn race, 1. a4 g5 2. a5 g4 3. a6 g3 4. a7 g2 5. a8/Q g1/Q, White is able to check first, 6. Qh8 +, which forces the black king onto the g-file (say 6. ... Kg6) for a winning skewer, 7. Qg8 + and 8 . Qxg1.

Pawn Roller An avalanche pawn attack. See STEAMROLLER and PAWN STORM.

Pawn Skeleton The general outline of pawns. So called because it's like a backbone, supporting piece placements and providing a foundation for planning. See PAWN FORMATION.

Pawn-Snatcher A PAWN-GRABBER.

Pawn-Snatching   Also called PAWN-GRABBING.

Pawn Storm   A general onslaught by pawns on one side of the board, as a "kingside pawn storm."

The idea of a pawn storm is to open lines leading to the other side's king. Also called PAWN ROLLER.

Pawn Structure   All aspects of pawn placement and dynamics. One of the five chief ELEMENTS of chess.

Pawn Weakness   A vulnerable pawn that can be attacked or can't be defended adequately by friendly pawns. Typical pawn weaknesses include DOUBLED PAWNS, ISOLATED PAWNS, BACKWARD PAWNS, HANGING PAWNS, and ISOLATED PAWN PAIRS.

Pendulum Draw   A draw by repetition when two attacking moves are repeatedly played and answered by two defending moves, with the same moves "swinging" to and fro. If the players do not agree to a draw, the game ends in a draw anyway by threefold repetition.

Perfect Information   A game theory term referring to instances where there is no hidden information.

Chess, for example, is a game of perfect information. Everything relevant could be discovered by observation if one's powers of discernment were sufficiently acute. This is not true for certain card games, for instance, where some cards can't be seen. There one has imperfect information and must rely on probabilities.

Permanent   Lasting throughout most of the game. Not subject to change or dissolution based on immediate actions and plans.

Permanent Advantage   A lasting advantage, such as material or pawn structure. The opposite is a TEMPORARY ADVANTAGE.

Permanent Weakness A square or pawn that can never be protected by a pawn, providing enemy pieces with a persistent target for attack. See HOLE and WEAKNESS.

Perpetual See PERPETUAL CHECK.

Perpetual Attack See PERPETUAL PURSUIT and PERPETUAL THREAT.

Perpetual Check A draw stemming from a series of checks that gain nothing but can't be stopped and that are usually initiated by a player who is losing or in TIME TROUBLE. Either the game is drawn by agreement or a threefold repetition eventually ensues. Also called PERPETUAL.

Perpetual Pursuit A drawing tactic by which an attacked piece other than the king can't be won but is unable to escape relentless threats of being captured.

W: Kc7 Bh5 Ps a3 d3 e2 g7   (6)
B: Kg8 Ra8 Ps a4 d4 e5   (5)

QUESTION: Can White play and draw?

Some perpetual pursuit examples are quite amusing. Even when there seems to be lots of room, amazing traps can suddenly emerge. See PERPETUAL CHECK and PERPETUAL THREAT.

ANSWER: White has a spectacular draw by 1. Kb7 Ra5 2. Kb6 Rd5 3. Kc6 Rd8 4. Kc7 Ra8 5. Kb7, etc.

Perpetual Threat   Two or more threats that can be alternated to prevent a superior enemy from making progress. A target is attacked, and when it's guarded the attack switches to a second target. When that's guarded, the attack shifts back to the first target. A draw follows. See PERPETUAL PURSUIT and PERPETUAL CHECK.

Petite Combinaison   A "little combination," usually leading to a small gain or a slight positional improvement. The kind of thing for which Capablanca was famous.

Phalanx   A group of pawns either advancing as an attacking force or standing side by side poised to advance.

Phase   A stage or part of a chess game with its own character. The three main phases are the opening, the middlegame, and the endgame.

Philidor's Draw In rook endings, a drawing idea based on a judicious third-rank cutoff of the attacking king.

W: Ke1 Rb5   (2)
B: Kf4 Ra2 Pe4   (3)

QUESTION: What is White's best continuation?

Black to play would advance his king to f3, so that no matter which check White gives, Black's king could find shelter. The most reliable drawing idea is to stop this invasion.

ANSWER: By playing 1. Rb3!, a third-rank cutoff, White halts Black's intrusion. White then draws by shifting his rook along its third rank. If Black continues 1. ... e3, trying to create shelter for the king to advance, White plays his rook to b8 for a series of checks from behind, and Black's king has nowhere to hide.

Philidor's Legacy A particular smothered mate attack in which the queen is sacrificed to block a potential escape square.

W: Kg2 Qf3 Ng5 Pb3   (4)
B: Kg8 Qb8 Re8 Ps f6 g7 h7 (6)

QUESTION: Where should White retreat the knight?

Philidor's Legacy has little to do with François-André Danican Philidor (1726–95). The idea actually goes back to analysis by Lucena in 1497. Philidor's name got mixed up with it in Thomas Pruen's 1804 book *An Introduction to the History and Study of Chess*.

ANSWER: The winning variation is 1. Qd5+ Kh8 2. Nf7+ Kg8 3. Nh6+ Kh8 4. Qg8+! Rxg8 5. Nf7#.

Philidor's Position In the endgame of king, rook, and bishop vs. king and rook, a winning position analyzed by Philidor.

Piece A king, a queen, a rook, a bishop, or a knight, but not a pawn.

Piece Play Activity with the pieces, especially minor pieces and rooks.

Pig   Chess jargon for a rook on the seventh rank.

Piling on   Exploiting a pinned unit by attacking it with additional force.

Pin   A tactic preventing or dissuading an enemy unit from moving off a line because to do so would expose a friendly unit to capture or a key square to occupation. The pinned unit is in the uneviable situation of being a shield. See ABSOLUTE PIN and RELATIVE PIN.

W: Kf1 Qf2 Rh2 Ps b3 b5 e3   (6)
B: Ka7 Qf7 Rf6 Ps a6 b7   (5)

QUESTION: How can White save his queen?

When your queen is seemingly lost in a pin it's easy to give up hope. But don't do that. Instead, find a tactic that turns the situation around.

ANSWER: White saves the queen by winning: 1. b6+! Kxb6 (1. ... Rxb6 allows 2. Qxf7, and 1. ... Kb8 is murdered by 2. Rh8+ with mate to follow) 2. Rh6, pinning and winning at least Black's rook! White escapes the pin by creating one of his own.

Pin Breaking   Ending a pin by putting a piece or pawn in the line of the pinner's attack, by immobilizing the pinner, or by capturing or driving it away.

Pin-Mate   A mate in which a key defensive unit is suddenly pinned and can't save the king by capturing the mating unit.

Pin Overload   Exploiting an overloaded piece by pinning it so that it can't fulfill its obligations.

Plan   A strategy. A general course of action.

Planning   The art of strategizing and forming long term goals.

Play the Board, Not the Man   A piece of advice suggesting that one should simply consider the value of the moves themselves and not the strength or rating of the person making them.

Some people play their best when they don't know the quality of the opposition; others play well only when the opponent is highly rated. But it's still wise to place emphasis on the objective qualities of the opponent's moves.

Plus   An advantage. Also, when given as a notational symbol (+), it means check.

Plus Score   An overall tournament result consisting of more wins than losses.

Ply   A term used by computer chess programmers to indicate how many half-moves a program looks ahead. Three ply means that the program looks at three half-moves, two for one side and one for the other.

Point Count See RELATIVE EXCHANGE VALUES.

Pointless Check A check given for the sake of giving a check. Like any other move, a check shouldn't be played unless it's a good move.

Poisoned Pawn A pawn offered as bait, the capture of which leads to trouble either because of a hidden trap or the time wasted capturing it.

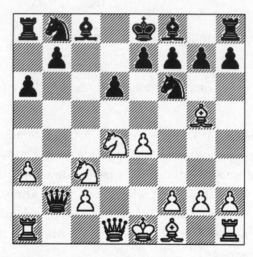

W: Ke1 Qd1 Ra1 Rh1 Bf1 Bg5 Nc3 Nd4 Ps a3 c2 e4 f2 g2 h2   (14)
B: Ke8 Qb2 Ra8 Rh8 Bc8 Bf8 Nb8 Nf6 Ps a6 b7 d6 e7 f7 g7   (15)
h7

QUESTION: How does White save the c3-knight?

To capture a poisoned pawn a player often has to position a capturing unit, play a second move taking the pawn, then play another move or two to extricate the capturing unit (possibly the queen) for consolidation. The loss of three or four tempi often leads to an untimely end.

ANSWER: White saves the knight by using it to trap the black queen, 1. Na4!, which had captured b-pawn.

Position The locations of all the pieces on the board taken together, either for one side or both. The term can also be used as a verb meaning to deploy.

Positional Concerned with long-term effects and not so much with immediate consequences; being careful while building for the future; playing to insure a slight but definite advantage.

Positional Advantage Any non-material advantage.

Positional Chess A style of trying to accrue small advantages without incurring problems. See ACCUMULATION OF ADVANTAGES and POSITION PLAY.

Positional Draw A draw agreed to for practical reasons, or a position that should be drawn. The attacker may have sufficient mating material but can't force mate because of the defense. See FORTRESS.

W: Kg2 Qb4 (2)
B: Kg8 Rf5 Pg7 (3)

QUESTION: Can Black move and set up a draw?

The problem for the inferior force in such circumstances is how to prevent the other side from realizing its advantage while keeping one's own force satisfactorily glued together.

ANSWER: Black holds by moving the rook to f6 and, as necessary, shifting it between f6 and h6, both of which are solidly protected squares. The rook is always safe and White's king is unable to join the fight. Logically, the game will end in a draw.

Position Play Playing for small but sure advantages instead of risky and unclear attacks. See ACCUMULATION OF ADVANTAGES and POSITIONAL CHESS.

Postal Chess Chess by mail. See CORRESPONDENCE CHESS.

Post Mortem Analysis of a game immediately after its completion by the players and onlookers. Loosely, analysis of the contest at any later point.

Praxis Practical play and application, as opposed to theory and analysis.

Prepared Variation An opening line prepared and analyzed ahead of time in an attempt to catch an unsuspecting opponent. See HOME ANALYSIS.

Preventing Castling A tactic or strategy that temporarily or permanently prevents the opponent from castling. See PREVENTIVE SACRIFICE.

Preventive Sacrifice A sacrifice to prevent the opponent from castling, keeping the enemy king in the center, where it tends to be more vulnerable.

Principle   A general truth serving as a guide for reasonable play. See RULE OF THUMB.

Principle of Two Weaknesses   An endgame concept advocating that a player whose opponent has one weakness should inflict on him a second weakness or target, usually at some distance from the first one, before proceeding with the final attempt at winning. Ideally, the opponent will not be able to contend with the threats to both points.

Problem   A tactical or COMPOSED PROBLEM. Any chess task with stipulations.

W: Kc5 Qe2 Bd7   (3)
B: Kb7 Ps a7 a6 e5   (4)

QUESTION: How can White force mate in three moves?

The above problem was published by Otto Wurzburg in 1895. The solution illustrates the Turton doubling theme, where the piece moved first is the one that delivers mate in the main variation.

ANSWER: White mates by 1. Bh3 (threatening 2. Qg4 and 3. Qc8#)

1. ... a5 2. Qa6+ and mate next. If 2. ... Kxa6, then 3. Bc8#; or if 2. ... Kc7, 2. ... Kb8, or 2. ...Ka8, White finishes with 3. Qc8#.

Problem Bishop A bishop blocked by its own pawns, a typical feature of certain openings. In the French Defense, 1. e4 e6, Black has a problem bishop at c8, which is already obstructed by the pawn on e6. A chief concern for Black is whether to exchange this bishop or somehow increase its scope. Also called PROBLEM CHILD. See BAD BISHOP.

Problem Child See PROBLEM BISHOP.

Prodigy A child under the age of ten who performs at adult-like levels. Famous chess prodigies include Paul Morphy, Jose Capablanca, Sammy Reshevsky, Bobby Fischer, and Judit Polgar. Loosely, the term is used to include talented adolescents.

Professional With regard to occupation, anyone who makes a living playing chess. Broadly, this may include not only players but also teachers, exhibitors, organizers, tournament directors, writers, vendors, and promoters. See AMATEUR.

Promoted Piece A piece that's been created by PROMOTION.

Promotion The advancement of a pawn to its last rank and its conversion to a queen, a rook, a bishop, or a knight. Generally referred to as QUEENING, even though UNDERPROMOTION is possible.

W: Kg1 Qe4 Rc1 Ps a4 c6 f2 g3 h2   (8)
B: Kg7 Qc7 Rd6 Ps a7 e6 f7 g6 h7   (8)

QUESTION: How can White force a win?

When a passed pawn is blockaded, the key is to break the blockade. Very often this can be done by means of a sacrifice because a new queen is in the offing to compensate for the sacrificed material.

ANSWER: After 1. Qe5+ f6 2. Qxd6! Qxd6 3. c7, Black can stop the passed pawn only by giving up the queen, which is tantamount to suicide.

Promotion Square The square on a passed pawn's eighth rank where promotion takes place. Also called the QUEENING SQUARE.

Prophylaxis A policy of playing to prevent, deter, or anticipate enemy possibilities. A Nimzovich favorite.

Protected Passed Pawn A passed pawn defended by another pawn and generally safe from capture, especially by the opposing king. Also called SUPPORTED PASSED PAWN.

Protection The guarding of a particular point with other units so that capture or recapture is possible there.

Pseudo Sacrifice An offer of material that isn't a true "sacrifice" because a favorable outcome has been foreseen. Often merely a step in a forced winning combination. Also called a SHAM SACRIFICE. See TRUE SACRIFICE and REAL SACRIFICE.

Pull A slight advantage toward one side, so that the equilibrium seems to be "pulled" in that direction.

Punctuation Comments Standardized symbols appearing after the notation of a move to indicate its quality in the opinion of the writer.

Symbol	Meaning
!	good move
!!	brilliant move
!?	a risky move worth trying
?!	a dubious move
?	mistake
??	blunder

Pure Mate The same as CLEAN MATE.

Push To advance, especially a pawn. Also, the advance itself.

Putsch A sudden attack by several pieces in a particular sector.

Putting the Question to the Bishop The move of a pawn to a3, h3, a6, or h6, threatening an enemy bishop that is attacking or pinning a knight. The move "asks" the bishop to either take the knight or retreat. Also called BIFFING THE BISHOP.

Puzzle Any kind of posed chess problem.

Q

Q   Abbreviation for QUEEN.

QB   Abbreviation for QUEEN-BISHOP.

QB-File   Short descriptive name for QUEEN-BISHOP FILE.

QBP   Descriptive abbreviation for QUEEN-BISHOP PAWN.

QB-Pawn   Short descriptive name for QUEEN-BISHOP PAWN.

QN   Abbreviation for QUEEN-KNIGHT.

QN-File   Short descriptive name for QUEEN-KNIGHT FILE.

QNP Descriptive abbreviation for QUEEN-KNIGHT PAWN.

QN-Pawn Short descriptive name for QUEEN-KNIGHT PAWN.

QP Descriptive abbreviation for QUEEN-PAWN.

QR Abbreviation for QUEEN-ROOK.

QR-File Short descriptive name for QUEEN-ROOK FILE.

QRP Descriptive abbreviation for QUEEN-ROOK PAWN.

QR-Pawn Short descriptive name for QUEEN-ROOK PAWN.

Quadrangle See SQUARE OF THE PAWN.

Quadrant A block of 16 squares making up one of the four sectors of the board. From White's perspective, the lower right quadrant cov-

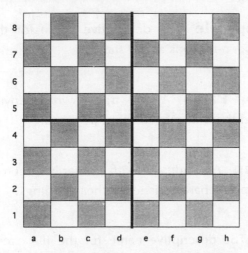

The Four Quadrants of the Chessboard

ers the area h1-e1-e4-h4; the lower left covers d1-d4-a4-a1; the upper left covers a5-a8-d8-d4; and the upper right covers e5-e8-h8-h4. Also, another name for SQUARE OF THE PAWN, as in QUADRANT OF THE PAWN.

Qualitative Majority A pawn majority with no weaknesses (no doubled or isolated pawns) and therefore capable of producing a CANDIDATE PASSED PAWN.

Quality The EXCHANGE; a rook for a minor piece.

Queen One of the six different types of chess pieces, symbolized by Q. It's usually worth the equivalent of nine pawns. Also, to PROMOTE to a queen.

Queen-Bishop The bishop that starts the game on the queenside (c1 for White and c8 for Black). White's queen-bishop moves on dark squares, Black's on light squares. Abbreviated QB.

Queen-Bishop File The descriptive name for the c-file, occupied by the queen-bishops at the start.

Queen-Bishop Pawn A c-pawn; a pawn occupying the c-file, whether it started there or moved there by capture.

Queen Ending An endgame with primarily queens and pawns, subject to the special characteristics of these endings.

Queen File The descriptive name for the file occupied by the queens at the start, known in the algebraic system as the d-file.

Queen Fork   A double attack or fork given by the queen.

W: Kc5 Qd4   (2)
B: Ke8 Ra6   (2)

QUESTION: How can White gain the rook?

As a rule, in the ending queen vs. rook it's usually (though not always) a bad idea for the weaker side to separate the rook from its king because of the queen's power. Winning forks seem almost inevitable.

ANSWER: The rook dies after 1. Qe4+ Kf8 (1. ... Kd8 2. Qd3+ or 1. ... Kf7 2. Qb7+) 2. Qf3+ Kg8 (2. ... Ke8 Qe2+) 3. Qg2+ Kh8 (3. ... Kf8 4. Qf1+) 4. Qb2+ Kg8 (4. ... Kh7 5. Qb7+) 5. Qb8+ Kf7 6. Qb7+ any 7. Qxa6.

Queening   Promoting a pawn to a queen. See PROMOTION.

Queening a Pawn   Same as QUEENING.

Queening File   A file occupied by a passed pawn.

Queening Square   The square on which a particular pawn is able to promote once it reaches the eighth rank, also called PROMOTION SQUARE.

Queen-Knight   A knight that starts the game on the queenside. White's queen-knight initially occupies b1, and Black's b8. Abbreviated QN.

Queen-Knight File   In descriptive notation, the file occupied by the queen-knights at the start. The b-file. Also written as the QN-FILE.

Queen-Knight Pawn   In descriptive notation, a pawn on the b-file, however it got there.

Queen on Its Own Color   An expression helpful in setting up the board at the game's start. When the board is placed correctly, with a light square in each player's near right corner, the white queen initially occupies a light square (d1) and the black queen a dark square (d8).

Queen-Pawn Game   A game that begins with a two-square advance of White's d-pawn. Also, any position that typically arises from games beginning 1. d4, however it developed.

Queen-Pawn Opening   An opening beginning 1. d4 or that becomes a queen-pawn opening by TRANSPOSITION.

Queen-Rook   A rook that begins the game on the queenside; it remains the queen-rook even if it moves to the kingside. At the start, White's queen-rook occupies a1 and Black's a8. Abbreviated QR.

Queen-Rook File   The descriptive name for the file occupied by the queen-rooks at the start; the a-file.

Queen-Rook Pawn A pawn on the a-file, regardless of how it got there.

Queenside The half of the board occupied by the queens at the game's start, including all the squares on the a-, b-, c-, and d-files. See KINGSIDE.

Queenside Attack A general assault on the queen's wing, usually directed not against the enemy king but for smaller gains (material, space, pawn structure).

Queenside Castling Castling on the queenside. After castling, White's king will be on c1 and his queen-rook on d1; Black's king will be on c8 and his queen-rook on d8. Written "O-O-O."

Queenside Majority An advantage in pawns on the queenside, often leading to the creation of an outside passed pawn, a DECOY. Also called QUEENSIDE PAWN MAJORITY.

W: Kg2 Ps a2 g4 h4   (4)
B: Kh8 Ps a5 b5 h6   (4)

QUESTION: How does Black play and win?

In most cases both players castle kingside, which means that a queenside majority is advantageous because it could lead to the production of a passed pawn away from the main theater.

ANSWER: The show closes after 1. ... b4 2. Kf3 a4 3. Ke3 b3 4. axb3 a3! and Black queens.

Queenside Pawn Majority See QUEENSIDE MAJORITY.

Queen's Wing The queenside, usually minus the d-file.

Quiet Move A useful move that is not a capture or check and isn't necessarily a threat in itself, but may contain a drop of poison. An unexpected resource, such as a ZWISCHENZUG. Also called a SLOW MOVE. See FAST MOVE.

R

R The abbreviation for ROOK.

Rabbit A player of some experience but little skill who thinks he's better than he is.

Race The rapid advance of competing white and black pawns to be the first to promote, or the race between a pawn to promote before the opposing king catches it. Also, any task requiring expeditiousness, such as development and maneuvering.

Race Game The oldest known type of board game. Any game in which one wins by being the first to either reach the finish line or complete a task. Backgammon is a race game, not chess.

Raking Bishops ALIGNED BISHOPS bearing down on an enemy flank, particularly the kingside, often from far away, capable of explosive attack. Also called HORRWITZ BISHOPS.

W: Kg1 Qe2 Rf1 Be3 Nd4 Ps c3 f2 h2   (8)
B: Kg8 Qd8 Rb8 Bc6 Bd6 Ps c7 f7 g7   (8)

QUESTION: How should Black save the c6-bishop?

Two bishops complement each other beautifully, cutting across the board as a unified force. When the center is open, defense against their combined assault can be difficult.

ANSWER: Why save the c6-bishop when there's mate in three?
1. ... Bxh2 + ! 2. Kxh2 Qh4 + 3. Kg1 Qh1#.

Rank A horizontal row of squares, of which there are eight on the chessboard.

Rank Beginner An absolute beginner.

Rapid Chess See RAPID TRANSIT CHESS.

Rapid Transit Chess SPEED CHESS played with a clock, a timer, or a bell. Sometimes it's played MOVE ON MOVE. Also called BLITZ, FAST CHESS, FIVE-MINUTE CHESS, LIGHTNING CHESS, or QUICK CHESS.

Rating A number, typically four digits, signifying relative playing strength. The FIDE RATING system is based on the work of professor Arpad Elo of the United States. See ELO RATING.

Rating Chart A table or list of USCF rating categories. The various classes are:

CATEGORY	USCF RATING
Master	2200 and above
Candidate Master	2000–2199
Class A	1800–1999
Class B	1600–1799
Class C	1400–1599
Class D	1200–1399
Class E	1000 1199
Beginner	Below 1000

Real Sacrifice The opposite of a sham or PSEUDO SACRIFICE; a material offering that entails risk because its consequences can't be calculated at the board, so the player must rely on JUDGMENT. Also called a TRUE SACRIFICE. See SHAM SACRIFICE.

Rear Attack In endgames, an attack by a king or rook from behind an enemy passed pawn.

W: Kf6 Be6 Pg5 (3)
B: Ke3 Be8 (2)

QUESTION: Can Black to play hold?

A rear attack is particularly efficacious for a rook. Though the king tends to be better placed defensively in front of an advancing pawn, blockading it, sometimes a game can be saved by menacing the pawn with the king from the rear.

ANSWER: Black draws by a rear king attack, 1. ... Kf4!, confronting the pawn and preventing White from posing a trade of bishops on f7.

Recapture Taking back after a capture.

Reciprocal Zugzwang A true ZUGZWANG for both sides.

Recording Moves See SCORE KEEPING and SCORE OF GAME.

Rectangular Opposition An OPPOSITION in which the kings stand at cross corners of an imaginary rectangle instead of opposing each other along the same rank, file, or diagonal. Also called OBLIQUE OPPOSITION.

W: Kg2 Ps e4 h3 h4 (4)
B: Kc5 Ps e5 h5 (3)

QUESTION: Where should Black's king go?

If Black plays 1. ... Kd4, White answers 2. Kf2, seizing the diagonal opposition, so that 2. ... Kxe4 leads to a draw after 3. Ke2. A possible continuation is 4. Ke2 Kf4 4. Kf2 e4 5. Ke2 Kg3 6. Ke3 Kxh4 (or 6. ... Kxh3) 7. Kxe4 Kxh3 (or 7. ... Kxh4) 8. Kf3 with a draw.

ANSWER: Black wins by taking the rectangular opposition, 1. ... Kc4, maintaining it until he wins the h-pawns, and then going back for the e-pawn. A sample variation of this idea, drawn from the work of Botvinnik, is 1. ... Kc4 2. Kf3 Kd3 3. Kf2 Kd2 4. Kf3 Ke1 (a TURNING MANEUVER) 5. Ke3 Kf1 6. Kf3 Kg1 7. Kg3 Kh1! 8. Kf3 Kh2 9. Kf2 Kxh3 10. Kf3 Kxh4 11. Kf2 Kg4 12. Kg2 Kf4 and wins.

Redactive Instruction A method of teaching that allows multi-move problems to be simplified by editing them backward from the solution.

For example, if the student has trouble finding a mate in five moves, the same problem is posed at a later point when there's a mate in one move. The problem may then be shown when it's mate in two moves; then mate in three; then mate in four; and finally the initial mate-in-five position is again presented. The technique, a kind of RETROGRADE ANALYSIS, stresses goal orientation while enabling inexperienced players to tackle difficult problems.

Refutation A move or variation that demolishes another move or variation. See BUST.

Refute To prove the unsoundness or incorrectness of a variation. See BUST.

Related Square Another name for CORRESPONDING SQUARE.

Relative Exchange Values The RELATIVE VALUES OF THE PIECES expressed as points, which are often calculated when considering exchanges.

Relative Pin A pin not involving the king and therefore allowing the pinned unit to move and accept the consequences. See ABSOLUTE PIN and PIN.

W: Ke1 Qd1 Ra1 Rh1 Bf1 Bg5 Nd5 Ng1 Ps a2 b2 d4 e2 f2 g2 h2   (15)

B: Ke8 Qd8 Ra8 Rh8 Bc8 Bf8 Nd7 Nf6 Ps a7 b7 c7 f7 g7 h7   (14)

QUESTION: Can Black win material?

The above position is a well-known trap in the Queen's Gambit Declined, arising from the moves 1. d4 d5 2. c4 e6 3. Nc3 Nf6 4. Bg5 Nbd7 5. cxd5 exd5 6. Nxd5?.

ANSWER: Black wins with 6. ... Nxd5!, simply moving out of the relative pin. After 7. Bxd8 Bb4+ (the sting) 8. Qd2 Bxd2+ 9. Kxd2 Kxd8 Black is a piece for a pawn ahead.

Relative Values of the Pieces The approximate numerical worth of the pieces expressed in terms of pawns or points and based generally on their powers and mobility in a variety of situations. Also called RELATIVE EXCHANGE VALUES.

The accepted values are: a pawn is worth 1 point, a knight or bishop 3 pawns, a rook 5 pawns, and a queen 9 pawns. The king has no exchange value, for it can't be expended. Of course, in any given circumstance a weaker unit could suddenly take on immediate significance (such as a pawn about to promote), but in most cases these values hold true.

Release of Tension   A pawn exchange, usually in the center, that tends to fix the game's character. The attacker prefers to maintain the tension by retaining options, disguising intentions, and delaying exchanges until a definite advantage can be derived. The defender often wants to clarify the situation by the release of tension.

Remis   French for draw, often used by pretentious non-French-speaking chessplayers.

Remote Corner   In certain endings, the corner most distant from the main fight, especially the one farthest from the pawns.

Remote File   In certain rook endings, the file on the edge that is most distant from the passed pawn.

Remote Passed Pawn   When each side has a passed pawn, the one farthest from the main theater, which can be used as a decoy to divert the opposing king out of position. Also, any passed pawn far enough away to worry the opposing king. See DISTANT PASSED PAWN as well as OUTSIDE PASSED PAWN.

Removing the Defender A tactic making a unit vulnerable by capturing, luring or driving away, or immobilizing its protector. Also called REMOVING THE GUARD or UNDERMINING.

W: Ke1 Re2 Bg2   (3)
B: Ke8 Re5 Nc6 Pb7 (4)

QUESTION: Can White win material?

Removing the defender usually means simply capturing a unit that protects another. If the first capture is a time-gainer (such as a check), the attacker may be able to take the undermined piece for free.

ANSWER: White wins a rook by exchanging bishop for knight with check: 1. Bxc6+ bxc6 2. Rxe5+.

Removing the Guard Also called REMOVING THE DEFENDER or UNDERMINING.

Repetition of Position Rule   A rule allowing a player to claim a draw by announcing that he is about to repeat a position for a third time. See DRAW BY REPETITION.

W: Kc1 Rb7   (2)

B: Kc3 Re8 Ps c2 c4   (4)

QUESTION: Can White play and draw?

The repetitions need not occur on consecutive moves but the position must be identical each time. The rule is usually invoked by the inferior side to avert defeat.

ANSWER: It's a clear draw after 1. Re7!, when the white rook cannot be taken because of stalemate. No matter where Black moves the rook, White will oppose it along the seventh rank. For example, if 1. ... Rf8 then 2. Rf7!. If Black doesn't agree to a draw White will eventually force a threefold repetition of the same position.

Resign   To give up before being checkmated, usually indicated at the bottom of a game score as "resigns." If White wins it may be scored as (1-0) and if Black wins as (0-1).

Resignation   The act of giving up before mate.

Restraint   The strategy, proposed by Aron Nimzovich, of playing to constrict enemy forces by overprotecting crucial squares to prevent freeing advances and reduce counterattack.

Retarding Sacrifice   A sacrifice to slow down or block enemy development. See SACRIFICE.

Retrograde Analysis   In problem composition, the process of ascertaining the moves that produced a given position.

Reverse Pin   Another name for SKEWER.

Reversing the Move Order   A technique in problem solving. It recommends that when you're having difficulty analyzing a sequence of two moves (or two ideas), as in a posed tactical problem, consider playing the second one first. Even if it fails, this approach may hint at the solution.

Right Bishop In the endgame (especially the situation of K, B, and RP vs. K), a bishop that can guard a friendly rook-pawn's promotion square, thereby averting a POSITIONAL DRAW.

W: Kc1 Bd6 Be4 Pa2   (4)
B: Ke6 Pf5   (2)

QUESTION: Which bishop should White save?

White could win a pawn by 1. Bxf5 +, but that would be a mistake, allowing a draw.

ANSWER: White should save the light-square bishop because it controls the a-pawn's promotion square. After 1. Bf3 Black could resign (1-0).

Right Corner In endgames where the defending king is better placed on corner squares of a particular color, a right corner is either of the two corners of that color. Generally, the corner offering the best defensive chances. See WRONG CORNER, WRONG BISHOP, and RIGHT BISHOP.

Right-Triangle Check An imaginary right triangle formed by three pieces (two kings separated by one square in the same rank or file, and one checking major piece on a line perpendicular to the line of the kings).

When the kings are on a file, the major piece checks along a rank; if they're on a rank, the check is along the file. In all cases, a right-triangle check drives the enemy king back a row, and along the edge it gives mate.

Right-Triangle Mate   A mate by a queen or rook along the edge, with several escape squares guarded by the friendly king. The three pieces trace an imaginary right triangle.

Roll   A sequence of forcing checks by two pieces of like power that drive a defending king to the edge or a corner.

W: Kh1 Qc3 Re8   (3)
B: Kd5   (1)

QUESTION: How can White force mate in four moves?

The typical roll is with two rooks, but a queen and rook are also a standard rolling force and, less often, so are a queen and bishop or two bishops.

ANSWER: It's mate after 1. Re5 + Kd6 2. Qc5 + Kd7 3. Re7 + Kd8 4. Qc7#.

Romantic Pertaining to a style of play distinguished by free-spirited attacks and a quest for beauty.

Romantic School Not really a school, but an approach to the game that was popular among players in the 19th century who tried to emulate the spectacular victories of Adolf Anderssen (1818–79) and Paul Morphy (1837–84). The style is typified by attempting to create artful sacrifices and combinations while striving for classical beauty and disdaining the cold logic of Steinitzian position play.

Rook One of the six different types of chess units. Worth five pawns on the exchange value market. Both sides begin the game with two rooks, each occupying one of the corners at the start.

Rook Ending An ending mainly with rooks and pawns.

Rook File Either the a-file or the h-file.

Rook Lift An advance of a rook, usually to the third, fourth, or fifth rank, to get in front of its own obstructing pawns so that it can shift horizontally to a more aggressive position.

Rook Odds A typical handicap, where the odds-giver takes the white pieces and starts without a queen-rook. In some versions of rook odds the a-pawn starts on a3 instead of a2.

Rook-Pawn A pawn on either rook-file.

Rooks Belong Behind Passed Pawns A maxim with particular relevance in the endgame. It recommends positioning a rook behind a pawn, whether in attack or defense, so that the rook's mobility will increase as the pawn advances. See BEHIND A PASSED PAWN.

Rooks Belong on Open Files A piece of opening and middlegame advice, recommending that rooks be positioned on files with no pawns in the way.

Round Robin A type of tournament where everyone plays everyone else.

Royal Fork A knight fork of a king, queen, and rook. See FAMILY CHECK and FAMILY FORK.

RP The abbreviation for ROOK-PAWN.

R-Pawn Short for ROOK-PAWN.

Rule of the Square A way to tell at a glance if a passed pawn can be caught by a defending king. See SQUARE OF THE PAWN.

Rule of Thumb A maxim or helpful principle, but not a rule as in "moves and rules."

Rules The laws of the game, as in "moves and rules," and distinguished from principles of good play. Loosely, principles and maxims.

Russian Exchange See RUSSIAN EXCHANGE SACRIFICE.

Russian Exchange Sacrifice Sacrificing THE EXCHANGE for active play and possibly to create a more aggressive pawn structure, often by positioning a rook where it is supported by two pawns so that a protected passed pawn ensues from its capture.

S

Saavedra's Position A famous endgame study, attributed to Fernando Saavedra (1847–1922), in which White wins by a clever underpromotion and a follow-up double attack.

W: Kb6 Pc6 (2)
B: Ka1 Rd5 (2)

QUESTION: After 1. c7 Rd6+, how should White proceed?

If White continues 2. Kb7, Black draws by 2. . . . Rd7, pinning the pawn and insuring its capture on the next move. If 2. Ka5, Black actually wins the pawn by 2. . . . Rc6. And if 2. Kc5, Black saves the day by 2. . . . Rd1, when 3. c8/Q? allows the winning skewer, 4. Rc1+.

ANSWER: White can force a win with 2. Kb5!, when play might continue 2. . . . Rd5+ 3. Kb4 Rd4+ 4. Kb3 Rd3+ 5. Kc2. Black then has the ingenious resource 5. . . . Rd4!, when 6. c8/Q encounters 6. . . . Rc4+ 7. Qxc4 stalemate! But not to be outdone, White instead plays 6. c8/R!, underpromoting to a rook and threatening mate. The only reasonable way to stop that is 6. . . . Ra4, but White then scores with 7. Kb3!, threatening the rook and mate at c1.

SAC Short for SACRIFICE.

Sacrifice A voluntary surrender of material for attack or other advantage. A GAMBIT is an opening sacrifice.

Sacrifice of Pursuit A sacrifice to force the enemy king into the open, where it can be attacked by at least several pieces and possibly driven into mate. See SACRIFICE and KING HUNT.

Sans Voir French for without sight, used in conjunction with blindfold play.

Saving Any tactic that avoids material loss, or manages to hold a difficult position, usually with a time-gaining threat.

Scheme A particular opening setup or pattern. Any such arrangement or plan.

Scholar's Mate A mate resulting from a typical beginner's mistake in the opening. White's queen captures Black's f7-pawn, supported by a bishop on c4, or Black's queen captures on f2, supported from c5. A favorite of school kids worldwide.

Two examples of it are: (1) 1. e4 e5 2. Bc4 Nc6 3. Qh5 Nf6? 4. Qxf7#; and (2) 1. e4 e5 2. Nc3 Bc5 3. d3 Qf6 4. Nd5? Qxf2#.

School of Chess An approach to the game shared by a group of players who are driven by a similar playing philosophy and who rely on openings likely to produce positions characteristic of this distinctive style. See SOVIET SCHOOL, HYPERMODERN SCHOOL, and ROMANTIC SCHOOL.

Score The record of the moves of a game; or to record the moves of a game. Also, a tournament result. For example, in a six-round event, if you win three games, draw two, and lose one, your overall score is 4-2.

Scorekeeping The writing down of the moves of a game. Also referred to as KEEPING SCORE.

Scoresheet A form with columns for the recording of White's and Black's moves, and designated places to indicate other information, such as the names of the players, the event, the opening, the date, and the eventual result.

Scoring The way the points are awarded in tournaments. Also, recording the moves of a chess game.

Sealed Move The last move before the adjournment of a game. Instead of being played on the board, it is written on the scoresheet, which is sealed in an envelope and revealed when the game is resumed.

Second In match play, an assistant who, before and after games, helps a player prepare openings, analyze adjourned positions, study the opponent's play for strengths and weaknesses, and oversee official tournament matters.

Sector Any subdivision of the board; usually an area where a particular skirmish takes place.

Seesaw A repeating double attack given by two line-pieces, a stationary one and a moving one, that seems to swing back and forth, like the motion of a seesaw. Also called WINDMILL and WINDMILL ATTACK.

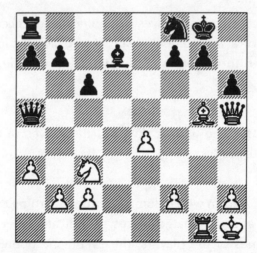

W: Kh1 Qh5 Rg1 Bg5 Nc3 Ps a3 b2 c2 e4 f2 h2 (11)
B: Kg8 Qa5 Ra8 Bd7 Nf8 Ps a7 b7 c6 f7 g7 h6 (11)

QUESTION: How does White save his bishop?

In a seesaw, two friendly pieces cooperate to fleece the enemy position. A stationary piece controls a crucial square, to which a moving piece repeatedly returns to give check and then moves away to capture something, discovering check by the stationary piece.

ANSWER: White regains the queen after winning a bishop and four pawns with 1. Bf6! Qxh5 2. Rxg7+ Kh8 3. Rxf7+ Kg8 4. Rg7+ Kh8 5. Rxd7+ Kg8 6. Rg7+ Kh8 7. Rxb7+ Kg8 8. Rg7+ Kh8 9. Rxa7+ Kg8 10. Rg7+ Kh8 11. Rg5+ Kh7 12. Rxh5 Kg6 13. Rf5.

Self-Block   A forced obstruction by a friendly unit, either by necessary capture or unavoidable retreat, that prevents your own king's escape.

Self-Mate   In problem composition, a situation in which White forces Black to mate him. Also called SUI-MATE. In ordinary chess parlance, the term indicates a game or sequence conducted so badly that it seems to be helping the opponent give mate. See HELPMATE.

Self-mate and helpmate are problem composition terms that are often confused. In a self-mate, White moves first and forces Black to give mate. In a helpmate, Black moves first, and White and Black conspire to mate Black.

Self-Pin   In problem composition, voluntarily moving a piece into an absolute pin. In ordinary play, it's usually an error—blocking a check by putting your own piece in a pin instead of simply moving the king off the line.

Semi-Closed   Descriptive of an opening in which White begins 1. d4 and Black does not respond 1. . . . d5; characteristic of INDIAN defenses.

Semi-Open   Descriptive of an opening in which White plays 1. e4 and Black does not follow with 1. . . . e5; characteristic of asymmetrical king-pawn responses.

Setup Check   A check that freezes the action or repositions a piece to prepare something else.

Seventh The seventh rank, often expressed merely as "the seventh."

Seventh Rank The seventh rank from either player's perspective. A great place to put an attacking rook. A rook on the seventh often attacks a row of enemy pawns while confining the opposing king and generally issuing powerful threats.

Seventh Rank Absolute A term used by Nimzovich indicating control of the seventh rank by a rook so that the opposing king is trapped on its home rank. Also called ABSOLUTE SEVENTH RANK.

W: Kg2 Rc2 Ps a7 f2   (4)
B: Kh8 Ra8 Ps g6 h7   (4)

QUESTION: How does White force a quick win?

In addition to harassing the enemy king, a rook on its seventh rank might attack several pawns. This is the row on which the opponent's pawns start and, even as late as the endgame, some of them may still be on their original squares. In chess slang, a rook so positioned is called a PIG because of its gluttony for these unmoved pawns.

ANSWER: White seizes the absolute seventh rank, 1. Rc7!. There is no defense to 2. Rb7 and 3. Rb8+.

Sham Sacrifice
A material offering that leads at least to a positional gain, if not an actual win. It's not a REAL SACRIFICE or a TRUE SACRIFICE because it lacks the element of risk: the player determines that it will have favorable consequences before playing it. Also called PSEUDO SACRIFICE.

Sharp
Aggressive; used to describe any move or variation with bite.

Shatranj
An outmoded predecessor of chess played in Islamic countries a thousand years ago.

Shish Kebab Attack
Another name for SKEWER.

Shogi
Japanese chess. A game in many ways similar to Western chess, since, like chess, it evolved from CHATURANGA and SHATRANJ.

Short Castling
Kingside castling, recorded as "O-O," often described as "castling short."

Short Game A game completed in no more than 20 moves; a BREVITY or MINIATURE.

W: Ke1 Qd4 Ra1 Rh1 Bc1 Bc4 Nc3 Ng5 Ps a2 b2 c2 e4 f2 g2 h2   (15)
B: Ke8 Qd8 Ra8 Rh8 Bd7 Bf8 Nc6 Nf6 Ps a7 b7 c7 d6 f5 g7 h7   (15)

QUESTION: How can White force mate?

The starting moves to reach the above position were 1. e4 e5 2. Nf3 d6 3. Bc4 f5 4. d4 Nf6 5. Nc3 exd4 6. Qxd4 Bd7 7. Ng5 Nc6.

ANSWER: It's mate by 8. Bf7+ Ke7 9. Qxf6+ Kxf6 10. Nd5+ Ke5 11. Nf3+ Kxe4 12. Nc3#.

Short-Range Piece Either a king or a knight, as opposed to the long-range pieces (the line-pieces): the queen, the rook, and the bishop.

Short Side A phrase, commonly used in the endgame, referring to the side of a pawn with the fewest files separating it from the edge. Also known as *short side of the pawn*.

A c-pawn is separated from one edge by two files and from the other edge by five files. Thus the short side of a c-pawn is the one nearest the a-file. The opposite side, toward the h-file, is the LONG SIDE. (Note that rook-pawns have only one side.)

Shot An unexpected tactic or a surprising resource.

Shut-Off A line block that prevents an enemy piece from controlling or using the line.

Simplification The process of exchanging pieces to avoid complications, emphasize a material advantage, get control of the position, and establish clarity.

Simplify To avoid complications and clarify the position by exchanging pieces.

Simul Short for SIMULTANEOUS EXHIBITION.

Simultaneous Blindfold Exhibition A simultaneous display in which the exhibitor plays blindfolded or with his back to the other players. The moves are conveyed, board by board, in chess notation.

Simultaneous Display Another name for SIMULTANEOUS EXHIBITION.

Simultaneous Exhibition A public demonstration in which a strong player contests a number of games at one time, each on a different board against a different opponent.

Sister Squares Another name for CORRESPONDING SQUARES.

Sitzfleisch A German word literally meaning "buttocks" and figuratively "perseverance." It describes the tendency of some players to just sit and wait out a tough situation, hoping the opponent will lose concentration and blunder. The introduction of the chess clock about a hundred years ago made this a less important skill.

Skewer A tactic by which a line-piece compels an enemy piece to move off a line, exposing another unit to capture or a key square to occupation. The opposite of a PIN; also called REVERSE PIN, HURDLE, or SHISH KEBAB ATTACK.

Skewer Check A skewer that is also a check.

W: Kb1 Qc1 Ne3   (3)
B: Kb4 Qf8 Nb3 Pa4   (4)

QUESTION: Should White's queen check at e1?

Black's chief problem is his badly placed queen, which is distant from the action and situated on the same diagonal as its king.

ANSWER: The game is won not by 1. Qe1+ but by 1. Qa3+!!, when moving the king to safety loses the queen, and taking the white queen allows 2. Nc2#.

Skittles   Offhand, casual play.

Slow Move   A QUIET MOVE. Also, a non-checking move, allowing the opponent a chance to defend or counter.

Small Advantage   An intangible advantage; one so apparently insignificant that the opponent sometimes doesn't even realize it is an advantage.

Some typical small advantages are control of an open file, greater mobility, fewer weaknesses, occupation of a strongpoint, and the better minor piece. Steinitzian position play advocates the accumulation of such small advantages, for eventually they could add up to an overwhelming advantage or a winning attack.

Smothered Checkmate   Another name for SMOTHERED MATE.

Smothered Mate   A mate delivered by a knight to a king blocked by its own forces. A familiar instance of this is PHILIDOR'S LEGACY.

W: Kh1 Qb1 Re1 Ps g2 h2   (5)
B: Ke8 Qb6 Ba7 Ne4   (4)

QUESTION: Can Black force mate by checking on g3?

The smothered mate in such circumstances has to be created by the attacker, for the defender is not going to block in his king voluntarily.

ANSWER: Black can't play 1. . . . Ng3+ because the knight is pinned. But he can mate by 1. . . . Qg1+! 2. Rxg1 Nf2#.

Sockdolager An old slang term, used often in the writings of Al Horowitz (1907–73), signifying a brilliantly winning move or daringly clever rejoinder.

Sound Correct and logical, said of a move, plan, variation, or idea.

Soviet School An approach to chess developed in the Soviet Union of the 1930s and 1940s, espoused in the writings of Mikhail Botvinnik and others, and pursued with professional vigor by a coterie of the Soviet Union's elite players. It advocates a clash for the initiative right from the start, driven by objective analysis of new ideas for sharpening the opening fight. Characteristic of the school is a spirited defiance of traditional principles, especially in the willingness, often at great risk, to accept structural weaknesses for active tension. A player of the Soviet school will entertain any idea that might work. Indicative of their individualism, few Russians admit that the "school" ever existed.

Space One of the major ELEMENTS of chess, evaluated in terms of MOBILITY or the number of squares influenced and controlled. The player who controls more of the board than the opponent has an advantage in space.

Space Count A way to determine spatial superiority by counting one point for every square in the opponent's half of the board that you either attack or occupy, comparing how many squares your opponent controls in your half of the board, and subtracting the smaller number from the larger. (If two different units attack the same square, score two points for that square.)

Spatial   Having to do with space, such as a "spatial advantage."

Spatial Relations   An aspect of intelligence dealing with space and its changing perspectives and orientations. One of the talents a strong chessplayer supposedly must have, though recently this has been questioned.

Speculative   Risky; often said of a sacrifice whose worth or outcome can't be determined with certainty.

Spite Check   A meaningless check given by a player about to resign, sometimes containing a SWINDLE, but usually played merely to extend the game or simply out of inertia.

Split Pawns   A pair of friendly pawns separated by at least one file.

Springer   The German word for knight, often used jokingly in some English-speaking chess circles.

Square   Any of the 64 delineated spaces making up the chessboard. Also, the board itself.

Square of the Pawn An imaginary quadrangle that includes a passed pawn. If the enemy king can enter the quadrangle, the pawn can be caught before it promotes.

W: Kh1 Pa4   (2)
B: Kf3   (1)

QUESTION: Can Black catch the pawn?

The "square of the pawn" is determined by visualizing a line from the pawn's location to the promotion square, here extending from a4 to a8. This line is one side of a quadrant, with corners at a8, e8, e4, and a4. In order to stop the pawn, Black's king, with the move, must be able to enter this quadrant.

ANSWER: Black stops the pawn after 1. . . . Ke4 2. a5 Kd5 3. a6 Kc6 4. a7 Kb7.

Square Vacation Clearing a square, usually by sacrifice, so that it can be used by a friendly piece. See VACATION.

Squeeze A situation in which it is undesirable for a particular player to be on the move. A position where neither player wants to move is a ZUGZWANG.

Stalemate The inability of the player whose move it is to make any legal move while not being in check.

Static Characterized by a resistance to change; lacking movement, such as a "static pawn formation." The opposite is DYNAMIC.

Staunton Chess Set The standard chess set design accepted and used around the world, named after Howard Staunton (1810–74). Also called *Staunton chessmen*.

Steamroller A menacing juggernaut of connected pawns capable of advancing and driving back enemy forces. Also called PAWN ROLLER.

Stonewall A particular pawn formation of mutually obstructing white and black pawns. For White the structure consists of pawns at d4, e3, and f4 (and usually c3); for Black, at d5, e6, and f5 (and usually c6). Also, in ordinary use, pawns at Q4, K3, and KB4 (and possibly QB3) for either side, without regard to the deployment of the opponent's pawns. See DUTCH STONEWALL and DRESDEN STONEWALL.

Stonewall Defense A black defensive wall, consisting of pawns at d5, e6, and f5 (and usually c6), typically occurring in the Dutch Defense (1. d4 f5).

Stonewall Formation A group of pawns occupying a player's Q4, K3, and KB4 (and usually QB3). See STONEWALL.

Stratagem A sudden twist or short tactic, usually played to improve one's position rather than to win material. Loosely, any tactic.

Strategic Having to do with STRATEGY.

Strategic Sacrifice A sacrifice to gain control of a line or square or to impair the opponent's pawn structure by inflicting weaknesses. See SACRIFICE.

Strategy The art of planning. General thinking, as opposed to the specific nature of TACTICS.

Strong Point A solidly protected pawn or square, usually in the center, that a player tries to maintain. See STRONG SQUARE.

Strong-Point Defense A defense based on a strongly supported center pawn.

Strong Square A well-guarded square, usually in the opponent's half of the board, capable of being occupied to advantage because no enemy pawns can attack it. See OUTPOST. Also, a STRONG POINT.

Study A composed endgame problem, often elegantly and economically artistic, hinging on one or more unusual, brilliant, or amusing themes.

Style A distinctive approach to conducting the opening and the play of the game. For example, a player with an attacking style often chooses aggressive but risky moves; one with a solid style develops quickly, attends to king safety, and takes few chances.

Subjective Tending to think in terms of one's personal preferences rather than the objective characteristics of a position. For example, not trading queens when the position calls for it because the player feels uncomfortable without the queen. See OBJECTIVE.

Sucker Punch   A last-ditch SWINDLE to save a lost game, usually consisting of both a direct and indirect attack. The hope is that the opponent will focus on the obvious point and miss the concealed one.

Sui-Mate   See SELF-MATE.

Supported Passed Pawn   A PROTECTED PASSED PAWN.

Supported Mate   A checkmate given by a protected queen on a square adjacent to the opposing king.

Support-Point   An ideal square to occupy, being well guarded by pieces and pawns. See OUTPOST and HOLE.

Swallow's Tail Mate   A mate given by a protected queen in which two of the enemy king's possible escape squares are blocked by its own forces.

W: Ke4 Qf8   (2)
B: Ke6 Qc7 Pe7   (3)

QUESTION: How does White force mate in two?

It's called swallow's tail mate because the overall pattern supposedly looks like a bird in flight (you have to stretch your imagination a bit).

ANSWER: It's mate after 1. Qf5 + Kd6 2. Qd5#.

Swimming   Playing aimlessly; without a plan; lost in complexity.

Swindle   A deceptive trap that, if the opponent falls for it, wins or draws an otherwise lost game.

Swiss System   A pairing method for tournaments. In each round, players are paired against opponents with similar scores, taking into account ratings and attempting to balance colors. The system is effective for large tournaments.

Symmetrical   Having a visual correspondence or a comparable setup.

Symmetrical Opening   An opening in which both White and Black play similar moves, though not necessarily in the same order. At the right moment, the player with the initiative, usually White, should be able to break the symmetry by playing a move that can't be copied without serious disadvantage.

Symmetrical Pawn Structure   A situation in which the pawns for each player occupy corresponding squares on the same files.

Symmetrical Play   For both players, moves and plans that are the same or similar and that produce a position with essential balance.

Symmetry   A mirror-image positioning of white and black forces so that the board could be cut into two perfect halves. Loosely, any kind of similarity that makes the position look balanced.

System   A set of related opening variations branching from a particular move or set of moves, in which pieces and pawns are positioned harmoniously and logically and from which definite middlegame plans emerge.

Szen Position   A famous endgame position analyzed by Jozsef Szen (1805–57) in which a king and three queenside pawns (W: Kd1 Ps a2 b2 c2) face off against a king and three kingside pawns (B: Ke8 Ps f7 g7 h7).

Tactical   Having to do with tactics (concrete attacks). The opposite adjective is STRATEGIC (having to do with general plans).

Tactical Finesse An unexpected resource that holds the position or enables a tactic or combination to work.

W: Ka3 Ne3 Ne6 Pe7 (4)

B: Ka5 Re8 (2)

QUESTION: Can White force a win?

White has to be careful in this study by M. Eisenstadt. If 1. Nc4+ Kb5 2. Nd6+ Kc6 3. Nxe8 Kd7 the pawn falls and White cannot force a win with just two knights.

ANSWER: The solution is 1. Nc7!, a winning tactical finesse, for 1. . . . Rxe7 encounters 2. Nc4#.

Tactics Specific threats, usually immediate and forcing. The opposite is strategy, the art of general planning. At the higher levels of competitive play, tactics and strategy tend to merge into an overall, systematic approach.

Take To capture. Also, a capture.

Take Back To recapture. Also, a recapture. When playing against a computer, it is possible to take back a move and play another. In this way, computers enable us to correct our blunders.

Take the Opposition In the endgame, moving the king into position to seize the opposition. If it's a MEANINGFUL OPPOSITION, doing so confers the advantage or holds the draw. See OPPOSITION.

Take Toward the Center When having the option of capturing with either of two pawns, theory generally recommends using the one that leads toward the center. The opposite is to "take away from the center," toward the edge.

Taking Away the Last Square In certain endings, guarding the very last square occupied by the enemy king along the edge of the board, thereby forcing it to move in the other direction toward an undesirable corner.

Tandem Together as a team. Also, the team itself, as in a "winning tandem."

Tandem Putback An older term for BUGHOUSE or DOUBLE BUGHOUSE.

Target A potential object of attack, either a vulnerable unit or square. Also, to aim one's attack at these weaknesses.

Tarrasch Trap Either of two traps in the Ruy Lopez attributed to Tarrasch.
    The first occurred in the game Tarrasch–Zukertort, Frankfurt 1887. The game went 1. e4 e5 2. Nf3 Nc6 3. Bb5 a6 4. Ba4 Nf6 5. O-O Nxe4

6. d4 b5 7. Bb3 d5 8. dxe5 Be6 9. c3 Be7 10. Re1 O-O 11. Nd4 Qd7?
12. Nxe6! fxe6 13. Rxe4 Resigns (1-0).

The second was played in the game Tarrasch–Marco, Dresden 1892.
That game went 1. e4 e5 2. Nf3 Nc6 3. Bb5 d6 4. d4 Bd7 5. Nc3 Be7
6. O-O Nf6 7. Re1 O-O? 8. Bxc6 Bxc6 9. dxe5 dxe5 10. Qxd8 Raxd8
11. Nxe5 Bxe4 12. Nxe4 Nxe4 13. Nd3 f5 14. f3 Bc5+ 15. Nxc5 Nxc5
16. Bg5 Rd4 17. Be7 Resigns (1-0).

Task A specific goal. In problem composition, a stipulation or set
of requirements to be satisfied in order to solve the problem. Also,
the problem itself.

TD The abbreviation for TOURNAMENT DIRECTOR.

Technique The method and manner of implementing a task,
course of action, or plan; the use of acquired skills, experience, and
knowledge to proceed efficiently and correctly while minimizing waste
and risk. The term is applied more to the middlegame and endgame
than to the opening, and often refers to actually winning a theoretically
won or holding a theoretically drawn game.

Tempo A move as a unit of TIME.

Tempo Move A WAITING MOVE. A way of transferring the turn to the other player—forcing him to move when he doesn't necessarily want to—without changing the position significantly.

W: Ke5 Pe3 (2)
B: Ke7 (1)

QUESTION: Should White move his king then his pawn?

White wants to play a TURNING MANEUVER to the sixth rank and occupy a CRITICAL SQUARE, but he can't because Black has the OPPOSITION.

ANSWER: So White should advance the pawn, 1. e4. Black's king will have to give ground and White's king advances to either d6 or f6, with an easy win.

Temporal Having to do with time, as in "temporal advantage."

Temporary Advantage An advantage, such as time, dependent on immediate circumstances, highly subject to change, and therefore impermanent.

For example, if you are ahead in development you must convert your superiority into a more concrete, lasting advantage, such as a material plus, before the other side catches up by completing his development. If, for instance, you use your edge in time to gain a pawn, you will probably keep that extra pawn throughout the game unless you make a mistake. A temporary advantage must be exploited at once, or transformed into something more tangible, else it disappears.

Temporary Sacrifice A tactic in which material is initially surrendered but regained with advantage. It's a sacrifice essentially in name only because the sacrificer knows before playing it that it works. See PSEUDO SACRIFICE and SHAM SACRIFICE.

Ten-Second Chess Speed chess played at the rate of 10 seconds per move. The players are cued every 10 seconds by a buzzer or bell or a tournament director's announcement.

Territory The portion of the board controlled by a player. At the start of play, White's territory is separated from Black's by the FRONTIER LINE.

Text In the printed annotations of a game, the text is the moves actually played as opposed to the annotator's alternate moves. In analysis, the text refers to the main line, exclusive of side variations and possibilities.

Text Move A move actually played and appearing in the main score of a game, not in the notes. Also, the primary move given in analysis, often distinguished from alternatives by a different typeface.

Thematic Consistent with, or relevant to, the dominant idea in a position.

Thematic Move A move that is consonant with the main concept of an opening or plan. Often the chief move in such schemes.

Theme The paramount motif in any chess situation; the chief feature of a tactic, problem, study, game, phase, plan, or method.

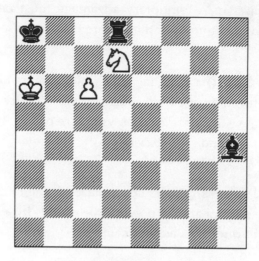

W: Ka6 Nd7 Pc7   (3)
B: Ka8 Rd8 Bh4   (3)

QUESTION: How should White continue?

The theme of the above 1962 study by P. Ten Cate is promotion. In three of the chief variations, White makes a new queen.

ANSWER: The winning move is 1. c7!. If 1. . . . Rxd7 2. c8/Q# (or 2. c8/R#); if 1. . . . Rb8 2. cxb8/Q# (or 2. cxb8/R#); and if 1. . . . Bf2 2. cxd8/Q# (or 2. cxd8/R#).

Theoretical Having to do with the analysis of critical positions, some of which may be speculative and therefore in need of further testing in serious tournaments and matches. A term with particular currency in the analysis of openings.

Theoretical Novelty A promising new opening move, possibly appearing in a notable game but not yet part of the accepted body of theory. An interesting or important move apparently worthy of further use.

Theoretician   A recognized authority on ideas critical to the state of the art, particularly in the analysis of new opening moves and lines, who publishes his work in scholarly journals for purposes of demonstration, evaluation, and either corroboration or refutation.

Theory   The collective judgment of critical literature on opening variations and systems, middlegame position play, and endgame techniques.

Theory of Corresponding Squares   Not a theory at all, but the concrete analysis of specific king and pawn endings to determine which pairs of squares are oppositionally related when there is no regular pattern. See CORRESPONDING SQUARES, OPPOSITIONS, and ZUGZWANG.

Theory of Critical Squares   A method to analyze king and pawn endings in terms of key squares that the attacking king tries to occupy and the defending king tries to control. See CRITICAL SQUARES.

Third-Rank Cutoff   In rook endings, placing the defensive rook on its third rank to prevent the invasion of the opposing king. See PHILIDOR'S DRAW.

Threat   A move presenting a danger that must be heeded.

Three-Dimensional Chess   A nonstandard version of chess played on three separate boards, usually stacked one above the other, in which the rules allow the pieces to move from level to level. This uses the form of chess played by Mr. Spock on the original "Star Trek."

Threefold Repetition   A rule mandating a draw if the same position is about to be repeated for the third time with the same player on the move.

The player must claim the draw before playing the move that will bring about the third repetition.

Newcomers often think the rule means that the repetitions must occur on consecutive moves (they need not) or that a draw can be claimed merely if the same move is played on three separate turns. The rule states that everything about the position must be identical: the same player must be on the move, every white and black unit has to occupy the same squares, and each unit must retain the same powers. See DRAW BY REPETITION and REPETITION OF POSITION RULE.

Three-Mover A composed three-move checkmate problem in which White plays a move and Black responds, White plays a second move and Black responds again, and White plays a third move, giving mate.

Time The period allotted for the playing of a clock game. More usually, the ELEMENT having to do with DEVELOPMENT and INITIATIVE. If you are better developed, or if you control the game's flow, you have an edge in time. Time is a temporary element, compared to material and pawn structure.

Time Control The last move of a time limit. A player must complete this move within the allotted time or forfeit the game. Also, the time limit itself.

Time Limit In a clock game, a period of time allotted for a certain number of moves. Failure to play the required number of moves in the allotted time—exceeding the time limit—results in forfeit.

Time Pressure The need to make a number of moves with only a little time before the time control. A player in such a situation is forced to play more quickly than he would like. Also called TIME TROUBLE.

Time Trouble   Also called TIME PRESSURE.

Timing   Playing a move or commencing an action at just the right moment.

Title   A recognition of achievement. The two highest titles awarded by FIDE are INTERNATIONAL GRANDMASTER and INTERNATIONAL MASTER.

TN   The abbreviation of THEORETICAL NOVELTY.

Touch and Move Rule   See TOUCH-MOVE.

Touch-Move   A rule, also called the TOUCH-MOVE RULE or the TOUCH AND MOVE RULE, requiring a player to move (or capture) the first piece touched. If a legal play with the touched unit is not possible, the player may make any legal move without penalty.

Touch-Move Rule   See TOUCH-MOVE.

Tournament   A contest in which a number of players compete. The ROUND-ROBIN and the SWISS TOURNAMENT are the two most typical chess tournaments. See MATCH, OPEN TOURNAMENT, and KNOCKOUT TOURNAMENT.

Tournament Director   At a tournament, a person empowered to enforce the rules, hear and decide disputes, post results, make pairings, and see to the smooth running of the event.

Toward the Center Toward the middle of the board. This is the usual preferred way to capture with a pawn when a choice must be made between taking away from the center or toward it. See TAKE TOWARD THE CENTER.

W: Kg1 Be2 Ps b3 d3   (4)
B: Kf8 Bd5 Nc4 Ps c6 e6   (5)

QUESTION: How should White recapture the knight?

How one takes back is not just based on general concerns. Of greater import is the tactical situation.

ANSWER: After the correct 1. bxc3, capturing toward the center, Black's bishop is trapped and lost. By taking away from the center, 1. dxc3?, White abandons central control and allows Black's bishop to escape to e4.

Trade An exchange of equal material. Also, to make such a transaction.

Transition A change from one kind of situation to another, or from one phase to another; for example, the transition from the opening to the middlegame. Also, the intervening period between two phases.

Transpose To arrive at a known or expected position by a different order of moves. In the opening, to achieve a standard position by an irregular sequence of moves.

Transposition A different or unexpected path to a given position, often taken to steer clear of unwanted possibilities. Also, the resulting position itself.

Trap A baited variation to lure a careless opponent into error. Also, to snare an opponent.

Trapped Piece A threatened piece that can't be extricated and is therefore lost.

Trapping The process or tactic of snaring an enemy piece.

Trappy Move A complicated, perhaps questionable, move that seems to be a mistake but actually conceals deceptive tactical points.

Trébuchet An endgame ZUGZWANG involving kings and fixed pawns, in which the player on the move loses.

W: Kd6 Pe5 (2)
B: Kf5 Pe6 (2)

QUESTION: Is it better to move first or second?

In French the word *trébuchet* signifies a trap or siege weapon. In chess it refers to a very common situation in which both sides must be wary.

ANSWER: It is better to go second. Whoever moves must abandon his pawn to the opposing king.

Tree of Analysis A schematic showing the course of a player's thoughts when considering candidate moves, with variations given as lines or "branches" of a tree stemming from one trunk. The trunk is the main move under consideration and the opponent's replies are the chief branches. These in turn can ramify further if necessary.

Triangulation An endgame king maneuver in which a player "wastes" a move to achieve the same position but with the other player to move.

W: Ke5 Pf6 Ph5   (3)
B: Kf8 Ph6   (2)

QUESTION: How does White win?

If White tries to win directly by 1. Ke6, Black holds the fort with 1. . . . Ke8. And if White tries to invade on g6 by first playing 1. Kf5, Black counters with 1. . . . Kf7.

ANSWER: White can break the pattern by stepping back, 1. Ke4!. After 1. . . . Ke8 2. Kf4 Kf8 3. Ke5!, we arrive at the original position but with Black to move. If Black continues 3. . . . Ke8, then 4. Ke6 takes the opposition and wins; while 3. . . . Kf7 runs into 4. Kf5 followed by 5. Kg6, winning the h-pawn. Another winning variation is 1. Kf4 Ke8 2. Ke4 Kf8 3. Ke5.

Triple To position three major pieces on the same line, especially the same file, so that the three form a triple battery.

Tripled Pawns Three friendly pawns occupying the same file. Usually a horrible weakness.

True Sacrifice A sacrifice involving a certain amount of risk because the outcome cannot be seen, unlike a SHAM SACRIFICE. Also called REAL SACRIFICE.

Try A move, variation, or possible defensive resource. In problem composition, a plausible move that fails against the most accurate defense.

Turning Maneuver A king advance to a CRITICAL SQUARE made after the opposing king has been forced to give ground.

W: Ke5 Pe4 (2)
B: Ke7 (1)

QUESTION: Black to play. What's the result?

If the superior side's king has the opposition in this type of ending (or comparable ones), it will have the ability to force a winning turning maneuver—so named because the king "turns" up the board to clear a path for the pawn.

ANSWER: White wins. If Black's king steps to d7, White's king has a turning maneuver to the critical square f6; if instead Black first goes to f7, White's king has a turning maneuver to the critical square d6; and if Black's king first steps back to the eighth rank, White insures a win by occupying either d6, e6, or f6 with his king.

Two Bishops
The advantage of having two bishops against either a bishop and knight or two knights. Also called BISHOP PAIR or *two-bishop advantage*.

Two-Bishop Sacrifice
A standard attack involving the sacrifice of both bishops to rip away the shielding pawns in front of the enemy's castled position.

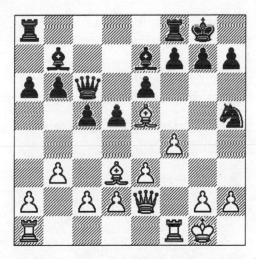

W: Kg1 Qe2 Ra1 Rf1 Bd3 Be5 Ps a2 b3 c2 d2 e3 f4 g2 h2 (14)
B: Kg8 Qc6 Ra8 Rf8 Bb7 Be7 Nh5 Ps a6 b6 c5 d5 e6 f7 g7 h7 (15)

QUESTION: How should White proceed?

The position comes from a famous game between Emanuel Lasker (White) and Johann Bauer in Amsterdam 1889. Lasker won by first destroying the cover in front of Black's king and then using the open kingside to threaten mate with heavy pieces.

ANSWER: The game continued: 1. Bxh7 + ! (sacrificing one bishop) Kxh7 2. Qxh5+ Kg8 3. Bxg7! (sacrificing the second bishop) Kxg7 4. Qg4+ Kh7 5. Rf3 (a ROOK LIFT) e5 6. Rh3+ Qh6 7. Rxh6+ Kxh6 8. Qd7 (a FORK), winning a piece.

Two-Move Mate A checkmate that is forced in two moves, whether in a normal tactical situation or in a composed problem.

Two-Mover A problem, usually a checkmate, that can be solved in two moves—two for the player on the move and one for the responder.

Unbalanced   Different but comparable. Lacking symmetry in the placement, kind, or number of forces.

Unbalanced Forces   Generally, different combinations of approximately equal but unlike forces, such as three minor pieces vs. two rooks. Also, comparable forces concentrated in different sectors, such as kingside vs. queenside deployments.

Unbalanced Pawn Structure   A configuration in which white and black pawns do not occupy all the same files. For instance, if one player has a kingside pawn majority and the other player a queenside one, or if one player has doubled and isolated pawns while the other has an equal number of healthy pawns, the pawn structure is unbalanced.

Unblock In general parlance, to clear a line by moving something, especially a pawn, out of the way; or to clear a space for the king so it won't get trapped. In problem composition, to vacate a square so that another piece can use it.

Unclear Uncertain as to the outcome of a position or line of play. Often used by analysts unwilling to commit themselves to a definite opinion.

Underdeveloped Lacking development; in the late opening or early middlegame, having several pieces still on their original squares. See UNDEVELOPED.

Undeveloped Having few or no developed pieces. Often used interchangeably with UNDERDEVELOPED.

Undermining A tactic to make a unit vulnerable by capturing, luring or driving away, or immobilizing its protector. Also called REMOVING THE DEFENDER or REMOVING THE GUARD.

Underpass A maneuver in king and pawn endings by which a king moves behind a passed pawn to reach the OUTSIDE CRITICAL SQUARE. Compare CROSSOVER and OVERPASS.

W: Ka1 (1)

B: Kc6 Pd4 (2)

QUESTION: How does Black force a win?

Most passed pawns are associated with a set of critical squares. The outside critical square is the one farthest from the defending king and therefore hardest to protect. Usually, the most effective approach for the attacking king is to head directly for that square.

ANSWER: Black wins by bringing the king to e3, the outside critical square for the pawn at d4. After 1. . . . Kd5 2. Kb2 Ke4 3. Kc2 Ke3 4. Kd1 Kd3 5. Kf1 Kc2 (or 5. Kc1 Ke2), the pawn can't be stopped.

Underpromotion Promoting to a knight, a bishop, or a rook, but not to a queen.

W: Kc2 Ph7 (2)
B: Ka1 Rg8 (2)

QUESTION: How does White mate in two moves?

Promoting to a queen is usual because an extra queen is a decisive force. But there are times when making a queen doesn't work. In the diagram, if White takes the rook and promotes to a queen, it's stalemate!

ANSWER: Correct is 1. hxg8/R!. After 1. . . . Ka2, White's newly created rook mates at a8.

Undouble To exchange off or capture with a doubled pawn so that the pawn formation is straightened. Also, from a line containing two major pieces, to move one of them off the line.

Unit Any chess figure, whether a piece or a pawn.

United Passed Pawns UNITED PAWNS that are also passed, so that either one has the possibility of moving toward promotion. See CONNECTED PASSED PAWNS.

United Pawns Two friendly pawns on adjacent files, occupying or capable of occupying the same rank, so that either one can support the other's advance. Also called CONNECTED PAWNS.

United States Chess Federation The official governing body for U.S. chess and America's representative in FIDE. The USCF's address is 186 Route 9W, New Windsor, New York 12550 (914-562-8350).

Universe For a passed pawn not on a rook-file, an imaginary section of the board consisting of the file the pawn occupies, the adjacent file to the right, and the adjacent file to the left. In theoretical king-and-pawn vs. king endings, the fight over the CRITICAL SQUARES generally takes place within this zone.

Unnecessary Pawn Moves In the opening, pawn moves that do not contribute to development. At other times, pawn advances that have no point or are needlessly preparatory.

Unpin A tactic for breaking a pin, either by obstructing the pinning line, by capturing or removing the pinning piece, or by moving the pinned or shielded unit, sometimes with a sacrifice to expose the enemy king and make possible a pin-breaking check.

Unpinning Combination Breaking a pin with a temporary sacrifice in order to follow with a check by the pinned unit.

W: Kg1 Qe2 Re1 Bc4 Nf3 Ps e4 f2 g2 h2 (9)

B: Kg8 Qb6 Rd8 Bg4 Nf6 Ps e5 f7 g7 h7 (9)

QUESTION: How can White win a pawn?

Unpinning combinations often hinge on a setup check to expose the enemy king. This may require a SHAM SACRIFICE (a sacrifice in name only) in which the sacrificed material is regained once the opposing king has become vulnerable.

ANSWER: White wins a pawn by 1. Bxf7 + !. If Black takes the bishop, White's knight first captures the pawn on e5 with check and then seizes the former pinner, the bishop on g4.

Unsound Incorrect because it can be refuted by correct play. Usually used to describe a variation that contains a flaw.

Up a Pawn Ahead by a pawn.

Up a Piece Having an extra bishop or knight.

Up the Board   Moving toward the opponent.

Up the Exchange   Having a rook against a minor piece.

USCF   The abbreviation for UNITED STATES CHESS FEDERATION.

Useless Check   A check that serves no purpose but is given for the sake of giving a check. Often the final move of a player about to resign: a SPITE CHECK or POINTLESS CHECK.

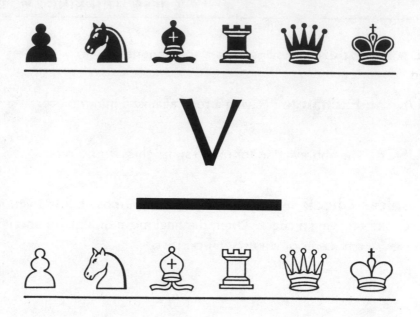

Vacate   To clear a square or line by moving a unit off it.

Vacation   Moving a unit off a square or line for tactical purposes.

Value   See VALUE OF THE PIECES.

Value of the Pieces   The relative worth of the pieces and pawns based on their mobility and powers, generally used to determine who benefits when an exchange takes place.

   Using the pawn as a comparative unit, knights and bishops are worth about three pawns each, rooks about five, and queens about nine. The king has no exchange value, but in the endgame, when it is most likely to be active, its attacking power is worth about four pawns. See RELATIVE VALUES OF THE PIECES.

Variation Any sequence of moves united by a logical, purposeful idea, either played in a game or proposed by an analyst. Also a specific opening line, such as the Dragon Variation of the Sicilian Defense.

Vertical Line A FILE.

Vertical Row A FILE.

Vertical Opposition Any opposition in which the kings are separated by one, three, or five squares on the same file. If they are separated by one square they stand in direct opposition; if by three squares, in distant opposition; and if by five squares, in long-distant opposition. See OPPOSITION.

Violation of Principle A transgression of a guideline or recommended course of play.

For example, a typical opening principle is not to move the same piece repeatedly but rather in general to develop as many pieces as reasonably possible.

Visualization The ability to see variations, positions, patterns, and applied concepts in the mind (without moving the pieces).

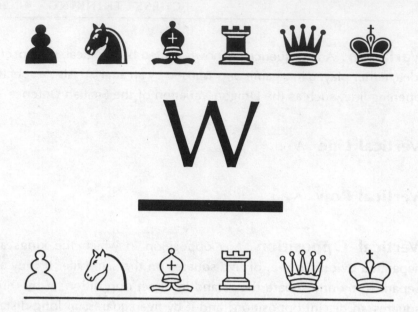

W

Waiting Move   A move that shifts the turn to the opponent without changing anything important in the position. Also called a TEMPO MOVE.

Wall   A controlled line. Any barrier to the king. Also, a shortened version of STONEWALL, referring to a particular pawn formation.

Wallboard   A DEMONSTRATION BOARD, especially one that hangs from the wall.

Walling In   A self-stalemating strategem to avoid losing.

W: Kh4 Ps g5 g4 g2 h3   (5)
B: Kc8 Ps a2 g6   (3)

QUESTION: Can White salvage a draw?

Walling in is a defensive endgame tactic. If you can't stop an enemy pawn promotion, or if you're simply losing a pawn race, try to block yourself up by "walling in" your king so that you have no possible moves.

ANSWER: White draws by 1. g3!. Black then makes a new queen, but White is left without a legal move: STALEMATE.

War Game   A type of board game in which one wins by capturing something. Chess is a war game whose object is to capture the opposing king.

Waste a Move   To play an innocuous move; to make it your opponent's turn mainly when it's undesirable for him to move. See LOSE A MOVE and TEMPO MOVE.

Waste Move A tempo shifter. A move played for no reason in itself, usually to compel the opponent's response. A waste move changes nothing essential about the position except whose turn it is.

Wasting Time Neglecting development, moving aimlessly, preparing unnecessarily, or pursuing the wrong plan.

Weakness A square, unit, or structure that's difficult to defend, especially because it lacks proper pawn protection. The term also applies to anything tactically vulnerable.

Weak Square A square that can be exploited or occupied by the opponent because it can't be guarded adequately by pawns. The weakness is pronounced if the opponent's pawns have a firm grip on the square to support invading pieces.

White The player who moves first and has the light-colored pieces.

White Pieces The light-colored pieces.

White Squares The light-colored squares. To distinguish between pieces and squares, regardless of their actual colors, the light pieces are called "white" and the light squares are called "light."

White to Play and Win A caption expressing a typical task in diagrammed problems and studies. Also given as *White to Move and Win*.

Most compositions are presented from White's point of view, with the white pieces moving up the diagram. The term "win" may entail either checkmate or simply a more-or-less forced sequence of moves resulting in a decisive advantage for White, such as being up a queen.

Widening the Front   In rook-and-pawn endings, increasing the power of a rook by a line-extending pawn sacrifice or pawn exchange along a key rank.

Since the rook's strength increases with the length of its attacking line, I often advise my students to get a rook on the seventh rank (a PIG) and then to "lengthen the pig."

Win   To defeat your opponent, whether he resigns or is mated (or forfeits on time). Also, a won game or a game that should be won if both players make the best moves.

Windmill   A series of repeating double attacks, starting with a setup check and continuing with a follow-up discovered check, resulting in the capture of material for free. The two-move sequence is repeated as long as desirable. Also called SEESAW and WINDMILL ATTACK.

Windmill Attack   See WINDMILL and SEESAW.

Wing   Another name for FLANK. The queen's wing consists of the a-, b-, and c-files, and the king's wing the f-, g-, and h-files.

Wing Attack   An attack directed against a flank, often as a counter to an enemy attack in the center.

Winning   Having an advantage that should win if both sides make the best moves. Also, forcing mate or producing a position that should eventually lead to mate.

Win the Exchange   To gain a rook (worth about five pawns) for a minor piece (worth about three pawns).

With Check   While giving check. Whatever the task, you can usually gain time by doing it with check.

Won Game   A game that with best play should end in victory.

Won Position   See WON GAME.

Woodpusher   A weak player. Someone who pushes "the wood" (or plastic) around aimlessly. See DUFFER, FISH, FISHCAKE, PATZER, WOODSHIFTER, and WOOD THUMPER.

Woodshifter   See WOODPUSHER.

Wood Thumper   See WOODPUSHER.

Wrong Bishop   With regard to certain endgames, a bishop that can't guard squares of the other color and so is unable to fulfil a specific task.

W: Kb1 Bc1   (2)
B: Kb3 Re3   (2)

QUESTION: How does Black force mate in two moves?

In situations of king, bishop, and rook-pawn vs. lone king, the wrong bishop is the one that can't guard the rook-pawn's promotion square. Since it can't force the defending king out of the corner, a draw results instead of a win. In situations of king and rook vs. king and bishop, the wrong bishop is unable to occupy either square adjacent to the corner of likely retreat and thus can't satisfactorily shield its king.

ANSWER: Black exploits the "wrong bishop" by pinning it, 1. . . . Re1. After White's king moves to the corner, the rook takes the bishop, giving mate. Move all four units in the diagram one file to the left and White suddenly has the "right bishop," insuring a draw because the pin produces stalemate.

Wrong-Color Bishop See WRONG BISHOP and BISHOP OF THE WRONG COLOR.

Wrong Corner In certain endings, the corner where the defending king is most vulnerable, usually because the corner square is the wrong color. See RIGHT CORNER and WRONG BISHOP.

X The symbol for capture. The "x" is given in lower case.

X-Ray A tactic by which a line-piece supports a friendly piece through a fully empowered enemy piece occupying an intermediate position on the same line. Loosely, any skewer attack or defense.

W: Kg1 Qh4 Rd1 Pg2   (4)
B: Kg8 Qb7 Rd5 Ps f7 g7 h7   (6)

QUESTION: Should White exchange rooks?

X-rays involve three pieces capable of moving along the same line: Two pieces of the same color bolster each other *through* an enemy piece of similar capability. In actual play, simple x-rays can be overlooked because our line of sight naturally stops at the enemy piece, oblivious of the squares behind it.

ANSWER: White scores with 1. Qd8+!, when 1. . . . Rxd8 2. Rxd8 is mate.

X-Ray Attack An x-ray enabling one attacker to support another through an intervening enemy piece—the most typical kind of x-ray.

X-Ray Defense An x-ray enabling one defender to guard another through an interposed enemy piece.

W: Ke2 Qd8 Rd2 Pg2   (4)

B: Kg8 Qa4 Ra8 Ps f7 g7 h7   (6)

QUESTION: Can Black avert mate?

Most x-rays are aggressive, designed to inflict damage on the opponent. But sometimes they are used to hold the fort when no defense seems possible.

ANSWER: Black saves the day with 1. . . . Qe8+!, blocking White's check with a check in turn (a CROSS-CHECK). White is forced to simplify to a losing ending (2. Qxe8+ Rxe8+), two pawns down.

Z

Zeitnot A German word meaning "time-trouble," now used fairly widely. See TIME PRESSURE.

Zero-Sum Game In GAME THEORY, a game in which a gain for either side means an equivalent loss for the other side.

Chess is a zero-sum game. In tournaments, exactly one point is awarded for each game. If there is a decisive result, the winner gets one point and the loser nothing. If the game is drawn, each player gets half a point. There are no additional benefits for triumphing in 10 moves or 20. It doesn't matter if you win by virtue of being ahead by a knight or by a queen. In the score column, you still get only one point for winning.

Zugzwang A German word meaning "compulsion to move." You are "in zugzwang" when any move you make worsens your position.

W: Ke6 Pd6   (2)
B: Ke8   (1)

QUESTION: Does White win?

Zugzwang refers to a situation in which you'd prefer not to move but it's your turn. Purists use the word to mean that neither player desires to move. A true zugzwang is a RECIPROCAL ZUGZWANG. It is distinguished from a SQUEEZE, which is a zugzwang for just the player on the move (if it were the opponent's turn, he wouldn't be in zugzwang).

ANSWER: White wins if it's Black's turn, but only draws if it's White's move.

Zwischenzug A German word meaning "intermediate move," also called IN-BETWEEN MOVE. It's usually a way to gain advantage by inserting a surprise finesse before following through on an obvious response, such as a recapture.

A. PANDOLFINI'S SHORT CHESS COURSE

■

MOVES AND RULES

THE BOARD: An eight by eight checkered board of 64 squares, 32 light and 32 dark.

LIGHT SQUARE RULE: Each player must have a light square in their near right corner.

ROWS OF SQUARES: Horizontal rows are ranks, vertical rows are files, and slanted rows of one color are diagonals.

THE PLAYERS: Chess is for two players. The lighter forces are called White, the darker Black.

THE FORCES: Each player starts with 16 units: eight pieces (one king, one queen, two rooks, two bishops, and two knights) and eight pawns. Queens and rooks are major pieces; bishops and knights are minor pieces.

THE OBJECT: To checkmate the enemy king.

THE FIRST MOVE: White goes first, then Black, then White, etc.

A MOVE: The transfer of a unit from one square to another.

A CAPTURE: The removal of a unit from the board by replacing it with a unit belonging to the capturing player.

GENERAL RULES: Move your own units. Capture your opponent's. Move one unit on a turn, except when castling. Move in one direction on a turn, except knights. Units move backward or forward, except pawns. Pawns move only forward. No move is compulsory unless it's the only legal one. The six kinds of units move in different ways. All, except pawns, capture the way they move. Only knights can jump over other units.

THE KING: Moves one square in any direction.

THE ROOK: Moves on ranks or files as many unblocked squares as desired, one direction on a turn.

THE BISHOP: Moves on diagonals of one color as many unblocked squares as desired, one direction on a turn.

THE QUEEN: Moves like a rook or a bishop, but only one direction on a turn.

THE KNIGHT: Moves one square on a rank or file, then two at a right angle, or two on a rank or file, then one at a right angle. The complete move looks like the capital letter L. It always covers the same distance. It can jump over friendly and enemy units, as if nothing were in the way. Each move, the knight moves to a square of the opposite color.

THE PAWN: Moves one square straight ahead. Each pawn has the option of advancing two squares on its first move. Captures one square diagonally ahead. Does not capture vertically.

PROMOTION: Pawns reaching the last rank must be changed into a queen, rook, bishop, or knight of the same color. No restrictions (you may have two or more queens).

EN PASSANT: Type of pawn capture. If a pawn is on its fifth rank, and an enemy pawn on an adjacent file advances two squares, the enemy pawn may be captured as if it had advanced only one square. The option may be exercised only on the first opportunity.

CHECK: A direct attack to the king, a threat to capture it next move.

IF "IN CHECK": A king must be taken out of check. It must be moved to safety, the check must be blocked (knight checks can't be blocked), or the checking unit must be captured.

CHECKMATE: When a king can't be taken out of check, the game is over by checkmate. The side giving check wins.

TO CASTLE: To move the king and a rook on the same turn. It must be the first move for both pieces. If the intervening squares are empty, move the king two spaces on the rank toward the rook and move the rook next to the king on the other side.

YOU CAN'T CASTLE: If you are in check or castling into check, or if your king must pass over a square attacked by the enemy (passing through check).

DRAWS: There are five ways to draw: stalemate, agreement, threefold repetition, 50-move rule, and insufficient mating material.

STALEMATE DRAW: A player is stalemated if not in check but without a legal move.

AGREEMENT DRAW: One player offers a draw, the other accepts.

REPETITION DRAW: The player about to repeat the same position for the third time may claim a draw by indicating the intended repetition. The repetition need not be on consecutive moves.

50-MOVE RULE DRAW: If 50 moves go by without a capture or pawn move, the player making the 50th move may claim a draw.

INSUFFICIENCY DRAW: If neither player has enough material to checkmate, the game is drawn. For example, king vs. king.

EXCHANGE VALUES: A queen is worth about 9, a rook 5, a bishop 3, a knight 3, and a pawn 1.

NOTATION: A way to write down chess moves. Pieces are abbreviated. King = K, queen = Q, rook = R, bishop = B, knight = N, pawn = P (if necessary). In algebraic notation, squares are named by combining a letter (for the file) and a number (for the rank). The files are lettered a–h, starting from White's left. The ranks are numbered 1–8, starting from White's side of the board.

White's king starts on e1 and Black's on e8. Some other symbols: check = +, mate = #, capture = ×, kingside castling = O-O, queenside castling = O-O-O, good move = !, bad move = ?. If both sides started by moving pawns in front of their kings two squares ahead, the moves are written: 1. e2-e4 e7-e5 (sometimes abbreviated 1. e4 e5).

PRINCIPLES AND GUIDELINES

THE CENTER Play for it. Occupy, guard, and influence it. Drive away enemy pieces that control it.

THE INITIATIVE White, having the first move, starts with the initiative. Be aggressive. Don't waste time or moves. Try to attack in ways that build your game. Combine defense with counterattack. Don't be afraid to gambit a pawn for an opening attack, but don't sacrifice without sound reasons. Don't waste time capturing wing pawns at the expense of development.

DEVELOPMENT Use all pieces. Move only center pawns. Aim to develop a different piece on each turn. Move out minor pieces quickly. Castle early. Don't move the same piece repeatedly. Develop with threats.

CASTLING Prepare to castle early in the game, especially if the center is open. Avoid weaknesses in front of the castled king. Castle for both defensive and offensive reasons (to safeguard the king and to activate a rook).

PAWNS Move both center pawns one or two squares ahead, preferably two. Make few pawn moves. Bad pawns moves create weak squares. Don't block center pawns by moving bishops in front of them. Don't move pawns in front of the castled king's position. Trade pawns to avoid loss of material, open lines, or save time.

KNIGHTS Develop knights toward the center, the white ones to f3 and c3, the black ones to c6 and f6. Develop them elsewhere only if needed or for a particular purpose (e.g. move the KN to h3 to guard f2). Generally move at least one knight before any bishops. Avoid getting knights pinned diagonally by bishops to the king or queen, or on the e-file by rooks to the king.

BISHOPS Place bishops on open diagonals. Use them to guard center squares, pin enemy knights, or defensively to break pins. Flank them if part of a plan to control squares of one color. Avoid unnecessary exchanges for knights. Use them to back up queen and knight attacks.

ROOKS Put rooks on open files (clear of all pawns), half-open files (clear of friendly pawns), or behind advanced friendly pawns. Double them, so that they support each other. Sometimes develop them by moving the pawn in front. Use them to attack the uncastled enemy king along the e-file and to pin enemy units. If feasible, place them on the seventh rank.

THE QUEEN Don't move the queen too early. Don't move it too often. Avoid developing it where it can be attacked. Don't use if it weaker units would suffice. Use it to set up multiple attacks, alone or in combination with other forces. Don't be afraid to trade it for the enemy queen if desirable or to avoid difficulties.

ANALYSIS Evaluate the major elements: material, pawn structure, time, space, and king safety. Elicit information about the position with probing questions. For example: Why did she do that? Did he respond to my last move satisfactorily?

PLANNING Plan early. Don't change plans without good reason. But be flexible. Modify your plan if desirable or necessary. Base your plan on an analysis of the position, noting strengths and weaknesses and accounting for definite threats.

THE ENDGAME Threaten to make new queens by advancing passed pawns. Force your opponent to surrender material trying to stop you. Activate the king. Trade pieces, not pawns, when ahead in material. Position rooks actively behind enemy pawns. Place them on the seventh rank. Don't tie them down to defense. With an extra queen, try to force mate.

B. OPENINGS INDEX

■

Abonyi Gambit	1. Nf3 d5 2. e4 dxe4 3. Ng5
Adorjan Gambit	1. d4 Nf6 2. c4 g6 3. d5 b5
Agincourt Defense	see English Opening (Kurajica Defense)
Alapin's Opening	1. e4 e5 2. Ne2
Alekhine's Defense	1. e4 Nf6
Alekhine's Defense (Brooklyn Defense)	1. e4 Nf6 2. e5 Ng8
Alekhine's Defense (Exchange Variation)	1. e4 Nf6 2. e5 Nd5 3. d4 d6 4. c4 Nb6 5. exd6
Alekhine's Defense (Four Pawns Attack)	1. e4 Nf6 2. e5 Nd5 3. d4 d6 4. c4 Nb6 5. f4
Alekhine's Defense (Modern Variation)	1. e4 Nf6 2. e5 Nd5 3. d4 d6 4. Nf3
Alekhine's Defense (Retreat Variation)	see Brooklyn Defense
Alekhine's Defense (Two Pawns Attack)	1. e4 Nf6 2. e5 Nd5 3. c4 Nb6 4. c5 Nd5
Aleppo Gambit	see Queen's Gambit
Amar Gambit	1. Nh3 d5 2. g3 e5 3. f4 Bxh3 4. Bxh3 exf4 5. O-O
Amazon	1. d4 d5 2. Qd3
Anti-Grünfeld System	1. d4 Nf6 2. c4 g6 3. f3
Baker Defense	1. e4 a6
Basman Defense	1. e4 g5
Battambang	1. Nc3 2. a3
Benko Gambit	1. d4 Nf6 2. c4 c5 3. d5 b5
Benoni Defense	1. d4 Nf6 2. c4 c5 3. d5
Benoni Defense (Czech)	1. d4 Nf6 2. c4 c5 3. d5 e5

Benoni Defense (Four Pawns Attack)	1. d4 Nf6 2. c4 c5 3. d5 e6 4. Nc3 exd5 5. cxd5 d6 6. e4 g6 7. f4
Benoni Defense (Knight's Tour Variation)	1. d4 Nf6 2. c4 c5 3. d5 e6 4. Nc3 exd5 5. cxd5 d6 6. Nf3 g6 7. Nd2
Benoni Defense (Mikenas Attack)	1. d4 Nf6 2. c4 c5 3. d5 e6 4. Nc3 exd5 5. cxd5 d6 6. e4 g6 7. f4 Bg7 8. e5
Benoni Defense (Old)	1. d4 c5 2. d5
Benoni Defense (Taimanov Variation)	1. d4 Nf6 2. c4 c5 3. d5 e6 4. Nc3 exd5 5. cxd5 d6 6. e4 g6 7. f4 Bg7 8. Bb5+
Bird's Opening	1. f4
Bird's Opening (From's Gambit)	1. f4 e5
Bird's Opening (Swiss Gambit)	1. f4 f5 2. e4
Bishop's Opening	1. e4 e5 2. Bc4
Bishop's Opening (Calabrian Gambit)	1. e4 e5 2. Bc4 f5
Bishop's Opening (Lewis)	1. e4 e5 2. Bc4 Bc5 3. c3 d5
Bishop's Opening (Lopez)	1. e4 e5 2. Bc4 Bc5 3. Qe2
Black Knights' Tango	1. d4 Nf6 2. c4 Nc6
Blackmar-Diemer Gambit	1. d4 d5 2. e4 dxe4 3. Nc3 Nf6 4. f3
Blumenfeld Counter Gambit	1. d4 Nf6 2. c4 e6 3. Nf3 c5 4. d5 b5
Boden-Kieseritzky Gambit	1. e4 e5 2. Nf3 Nf6 3. Bc4 Nxe4 4. Nc3
Budapest Defense	1. d4 Nf6 2. c4 e5
Budapest Defense (Balogh Gambit)	1. d4 Nf6 2. c4 e5 3. dxe5 Ng4 4. e4 d6
Budapest Defense (Fajarowicz Variation)	1. d4 Nf6 2. c4 e5 3. dxe5 Ne4
Bugayev Attack	1. b4, 2. a3
Caro-Kann Defense	1. e4 c6 2. d4 d5
Caro-Kann Defense (Advance Variation)	1. e4 c6 2. d4 d5 3. e5
Caro-Kann Defense (Bronstein-Larsen Variation)	1. e4 c6 2. d4 d5 3. Nc3 dxe4 4. Nxe4 Nf6 5. Nxf6+ gxf6
Caro-Kann Defense (Edinburgh Variation)	1. e4 c6 2. d4 d5 3. Nd2 Qb6

Caro-Kann Defense (Exchange Variation)	1. e4 c6 2. d4 d5 3. exd5 cxd5
Caro-Kann Defense (Fantasy Variation)	1. e4 c6 2. d4 d5 3. f3
Caro-Kann Defense (Goldman Variation)	1. e4 c6 2. Nc3 d5 3. Qf3
Caro-Kann Defense (Gurgenidze Variation)	1. e4 c6 2. d4 d5 3. Nc3 g6
Caro-Kann Defense (Main Line)	1. e4 c6 2. d4 d5 3. Nc3 dxe4 4. Nxe4 Bf5
Caro-Kann Defense (New)	1. e4 c6 2. d4 d5 3. Nd2 g6
Caro-Kann Defense (Panov Attack)	1. e4 c6 2. d4 d5 3. exd5 cxd5 4. c4
Caro-Kann Defense (Two Knights Variation)	1. e4 c6 2. Nc3 d5 3. Nf3
Catalan Opening	1. d4 Nf6 2. c4 e6 3. g3 d5
Catalan Opening (Classical Line)	1. d4 Nf6 2. c4 e6 3. g3 d5 4. Bg2 dxc4 5. Nf3 Be7
Catalan Opening (Closed Variation)	1. d4 Nf6 2. c4 e6 3. g3 d5 4. Bg2 Be7 5. Nf3 O-O 6. O-O
Catalan Opening (Open Variation)	1. d4 Nf6 2. c4 e6 3. g3 d5 4. Bg2 dxc4
Center Counter Defense	1. e4 d5
Center Counter Defense (Icelandic)	1. e4 d5 2. exd5 Nf6 3. c4 e6
Center Counter Defense (Mieses-Kotrc Gambit)	1. e4 d5 2. exd5 Qxd5 3. Nc3 Qa5 4. b4
Center Counter Defense (Scandinavian Gambit)	1. e4 d5 2. exd5 Nf6 3. c4 c6
Center Game	1. e4 e5 2. d4 exd4 3. Qxd4
Charlick-Englund Gambit	1. d4 e5
Colle System	1. d4, 2. Nf3, 3. e3, 4. Bd3, 5. c3, 6. O-O, 7. Nbd2
Colorado Counter	1. e4 Nc6 2. Nf3 f5
Dada Gambit	1. g3 e5 2. Bg2 d5 3. b4
Damiano's Defense	1. e4 e5 2. Nf3 f6
Danish Gambit	1. e4 e5 2. d4 exd4 3. c3
Dory Defense	1. d4 Nf6 2. Nf3 e6 3. e3 Ne4
Double Fianchetto Attack	b3, Bb2, g3, Bg2

Dunst	1. Nc3
Dutch Defense	1. d4 f5
Dutch Defense (Balogh's Defense)	1. d4 f5 2. e4 d6
Dutch Defense (Classical System)	1. d4 f5 2. g3 Nf6 3. Bg2 e6
Dutch Defense (Ilyin-Genevsky System)	1. d4 f5 2. g3 Nf6 3. Bg2 e6 4. c4 Be7 5. Nf3 O-O 6. O-O d6
Dutch Defense (Korchnoi Attack)	1. d4 f5 2. h3
Dutch Defense (Krejcik Gambit)	1. d4 f5 2. g4
Dutch Defense (Leningrad Variation)	1. d4 f5 2. c4 Nf6 3. g3 g6 4. Bg2 Bg7
Dutch Defense (Manhattan Variation)	1. d4 f5 2. Qd3
Dutch Defense (Nimzo-Indian)	1. d4 f5 2. c4 Nf6 3. Nf3 e6 4. Nc3 Bb4
Dutch Defense (Reversed)	1. f4 d5
Dutch Defense (Sjodin)	1. d4 e6 2. Nf3 f5 3. e4
Dutch Defense (Spielmann Gambit)	1. d4 f5 2. Nc3 Nf6 3. g4
Dutch Defense (Staunton Gambit)	1. d4 f5 2. e4
Dutch Defense (Stonewall Formation)	1. d4 f5 2. c4 Nf6 3. g3 e6 4. Bg2 Be7 5. Nf3 O-O 6. O-O d5
Dzin	1. d4 Nf6 2. c4 e6 3. Nf3 a6
Elephant Gambit	1. e4 e5 2. Nf3 d5
English Defense	1. d4 e6 2. c4 b6 3. e4 Bb7
English Opening	1. c4
English Opening (Accelerated Fianchetto)	see English Opening (Carls' Bremen System)
English Opening (Adorjan Defense)	1. c4 g6 2. e4 e5
English Opening (Anglo-Polish Dutch)	1. c4 f5 2. b4
English Opening (Anglo-Slav)	1. c4 c6
English Opening (Basmaniac Gambit)	1. c4 c5 2. Nf3 h6

English Opening (Bellon Gambit)	1. c4 e5 2. Nc3 Nf6 3. Nf3 e4 4. Ng5 b5
English Opening (Carls' Bremen System)	1. c4 e5 2. Nc3 Nf6 3. g3
English Opening (Closed Variation)	1. c4 e5 2. Nc3 Nc6 3. g3 g6 4. Bg2 Bg7
English Opening (Double Fianchetto Defense)	1. c4 Nf6 2. Nf3 b6 3. g3 Bb7 4. Bg2 c5 5. O-O g6
English Opening (English Defense)	1. c4 b6 2. d4 e6
English Opening (Fischer's Gambit)	1. c4 e5 2. Nc3 Nc6 3. g3 f5 4. Bg2 Nf6 5. d3 Bc5 6. e3 f4
English Opening (Four Knights Variation)	1. c4 e5 2. Nc3 Nf6 3. Nf3 Nc6
English Opening (Great Snake)	1. c4 g6
English Opening (Grünfeld)	1. c4 Nf6 2. Nc3 d5
English Opening (Hedgehog Defense)	1. c4 c5 2. Nf3 Nf6 3. Nc3 e6 4. g3 b6
English Opening (Keres Defense)	1. c4 c5 2. Nf3 Nf6 3. Nc3 e6 4. g3 d5 5. cxd5 Nxd5 6. Bg2 Nc6 7. O-O Be7
English Opening (Keres Variation)	1. c4 e5 2. Nc3 Nf6 3. g3 c6
English Opening (King's Indian)	1. c4 Nf6 2. Nc3 g6 3. g3 Bg7 4. Bg2 O-O
English Opening (Kurajica Defense)	1. c4 e6 2. Nf3 d5 3. g3 c6
English Opening (Nimzo-Indian)	1. c4 Nf6 2. Nc3 e6 3. Nf3 Bb4
English Opening (Orangutan)	1. c4 Nf6 2. b4
English Opening (Queen's Indian)	1. c4 Nf6 2. Nc3 e6 3. Nf3 b6
English Opening (Romanishin Variation)	1. c4 Nf6 2. Nf3 e6 3. g3 a6 4. Bg2 b5
English Opening (Rubinstein/Botvinnik Variation)	1. c4 c5 2. Nc3 Nf6 3. g3 d5 4. cxd5 Nxd5 5. Bg2 Nc7
English Opening (Slav Defense)	1. c4 Nf6 2. Nc3 c6

English Opening (Symmetrical Four Knights)	1. c4 c5 2. Nf3 Nf6 3. Nc3 Nc6
English Opening (Symmetrical Variation)	1. c4 c5
English Opening (Ultra-Symmetrical)	1. c4 c5 2. Nc3 Nc6 3. g3 g6 4. Bg2 Bg7
Englund Gambit	see Charlick Englund Gambit
Four Knights Game	1. e4 e5 2. Nf3 Nc6 3. Nc3 Nf6
Four Knights Game (Belgrade Gambit)	1. e4 e5 2. Nf3 Nc6 3. Nc3 Nf6 4. d4 exd4 5. Nd5
Four Knights Game (Rubinstein Variation)	1. e4 e5 2. Nf3 Nc6 3. Nc3 Nf6 4. Bb5 Nd4
Four Knights Game (Scotch)	1. e4 e5 2. Nf3 Nc6 3. Nc3 Nf6 4. d4
Four Knights Game (Spanish)	1. e4 e5 2. Nf3 Nc6 3. Nc3 Nf6 4. Bb5
Four Knights Game (Svenonius Variation)	1. e4 e5 2. Nf3 Nc6 3. Nc3 Nf6 4. Bb5 Bb4 5. O-O O-O 6. d3 Bxc3 7. bxc3 d5
Four Knights Game (Symmetrical Variation)	1. e4 e5 2. Nf3 Nc6 3. Nc3 Nf6 4. Bb5 Bb4 5. O-O O-O 6. d3 d6
Franco-Indian Defense	1. d4 e6 2. c4 Bb4 +
French Defense	1. e4 e6
French Defense (Advance Variation)	1. e4 e6 2. d4 d5 3. e5
French Defense (Alekhine-Chatard Attack)	1. e4 e6 2. d4 d5 3. Nc3 Nf6 4. Bg5 Be7 5. e5 Nfd7 6. h4
French Defense (Burn Variation)	1. e4 e6 2. d4 d5 3. Nc3 Nf6 4. Bg5 dxe4
French Defense (Chigorin Variation)	1. e4 e6 2. Qe2
French Defense (Classical Variation)	1. e4 e6 2. d4 d5 3. Nc3 Nf6 4. Bg5 Be7
French Defense (Exchange Variation)	1. e4 e6 2. d4 d5 3. exd5 exd5
French Defense (Extended Bishop Swap)	1. e4 e6 2. d4 d5 3. e5 c5 4. c3 Qb6 5. Nf3 Bd7 6. Be2 Bb5
French Defense (Franco-Benoni)	1. e4 e6 2. d4 c5 3. d5
French Defense (Guimard Variation)	1. e4 e6 2. d4 d5 3. Nd2 Nc6

French Defense (MacCutcheon Variation)	1. e4 e6 2. d4 d5 3. Nc3 Nf6 4. Bg5 Bb4
French Defense (Marshall Defense)	1. e4 e6 2. d4 d5 3. Nc3 c5
French Defense (Milner-Barry Gambit)	1. e4 e6 2. d4 d5 3. e5 c5 4. c3 Nc6 5. Nf3 Qb6 6. Bd3 cxd4 7. cxd4 Bd7 8. O-O Nxd4 9. Nxd4 Qxd4
French Defense (Reti)	1. e4 e6 2. b3
French Defense (Reversed Philidor)	1. e4 e6 2. d3 d5 3. Nd2 Nf6 4. Ngf3 Nc6 5. Be2
French Defense (Rubinstein Variation)	1. e4 e6 2. d4 d5 3. Nc3 dxe4
French Defense (Steinitz Attack)	1. e4 e6 2. e5
French Defense (Steinitz Variation)	1. e4 e6 2. d4 d5 3. Nc3 Nf6 4. e5
French Defense (Tarrasch Variation)	1. e4 e6 2. d4 d5 3. Nd2
French Defense (Two Knights Variation)	1. e4 e6 2. Nf3 d5 3. Nc3
French Defense (Winawer Variation)	1. e4 e6 2. d4 d5 3. Nc3 Bb4
French Defense (Winawer Variation-poisoned pawn)	1. e4 e6 2. d4 d5 3. Nc3 Bb4 4. e5 c5 5. a3 Bxc3+ 6. bxc3 Ne7 7. Qg4 Qc7 8. Qxg7 Rg8 9. Qxh7 cxd4
French Defense (Wing Gambit)	1. e4 e6 2. Nf3 d5 3. e5 c5 4. b4
From's Gambit Reversed	1. Nc3 f5 2. e4 fxe4 3. d3
Giuoco Piano	1. e4 e5 2. Nf3 Nc6 3. Bc4 Bc5
Giuoco Piano (Canal Variation)	1. e4 e5 2. Nf3 Nc6 3. Bc4 Bc5 4. d3 Nf6 5. Nc3 d6 6. Bg5
Giuoco Piano (Cracow Variation)	1. e4 e5 2. Nf3 Nc6 3. Bc4 Bc5 4. c3 Nf6 5. d4 exd4 6. cxd4 Bb4+ 7. Kf1
Giuoco Piano (Evans Gambit)	1. e4 e5 2. Nf3 Nc6 3. Bc4 Bc5 4. b4
Giuoco Piano (Evans Gambit-Compromised Defense)	1. e4 e5 2. Nf3 Nc6 3. Bc4 Bc5 4. b4 Bxb4 5. c3 Ba5 6. d4 exd4 7. O-O dxc3
Giuoco Piano (Moller Attack)	1. e4 e5 2. Nf3 Nc6 3. Bc4 Bc5 4. c3 Nf6 5. d4 exd4 6. cxd4 Bb4+ 7. Nc3 Nxe4 8. O-O Bxc3 9. d5
Giuoco Piano (Pianissimo)	1. e4 e5 2. Nf3 Nc6 3. Bc4 Bc5 4. c3 Nf6 5. d3

Giuoco Piano (Rousseau)	1. e4 e5 2. Nf3 Nc6 3. Bc4 f5
Grob	see Spike
Grünfeld Defense	1. d4 Nf6 2. c4 g6 3. Nc3 d5
Grünfeld Defense (Classical Line)	1 d4 Nf6 2. c4 g6 3. Nc3 d5 4. Nf3 Bg7 5. Qb3 dxc4 6. Qxc4 O-O 7. e4
Grünfeld Defense (Exchange Variation)	1. d4 Nf6 2. c4 g6 3. Nc3 d5 4. cxd5 Nxd5 5. e4
Grünfeld Defense (Neo-Grünfeld)	1. d4 Nf6 2. c4 g6 3. g3 Bg7 4. Bg2 d5
Grünfeld Defense (Prins Variation)	1. d4 Nf6 2. c4 g6 3. Nc3 d5 4. Nf3 Bg7 5. Qb3 dxc4 6. Qxc4 O-O 7. e4 Na6
Grünfeld Defense (Reversed)	1. Nf3 d5 2. g3 c5 3. Bg2 Nc6 4. d4
Grünfeld Defense (Smyslov Variation)	1. d4 Nf6 2. c4 g6 3. Nc3 d5 4. Nf3 Bg7 5. Qb3 dxc4 6. Qxc4 O-O 7. e4 Bg4
Guatemala Defense	1. e4 b6 2. d4 Ba6
Heinrich Wagner Gambit	1. d4 Nf6 2. Nf3 e6 3. Bg5 c5 4. e4
Hippopotamus	. . . g6, . . . f6, . . . e6, . . . d6
Italian Opening	1. e4 e5 2. Nf3 Nc6 3. Bc4
Keres Defense	1. d4 e6 2. c4 Bb4+
Kevitz-Trajkovic Defense	see Black Knights' Tango
King's Fianchetto Defense	1. d4 g6
King's Gambit	1. e4 e5 2. f4
King's Gambit (Accepted)	1. e4 e5 2. f4 exf4
King's Gambit (Algaier Gambit)	1. e4 e5 2. f4 exf4 3. Nf3 g5 4. h4 g4 5. Ng5
King's Gambit (Bertin)	1. e4 e5 2. f4 exf4 3. Nf3 Be7 4. Bc4 Bh4+ 5. g3
King's Gambit (Breyer Gambit)	1. e4 e5 2. f4 exf4 3. Qf3
King's Gambit (Bryan)	1. e4 e5 2. f4 exf4 3. Bc4 Qh4+ 4. Kf1 b5
King's Gambit (Cunningham Variation)	1. e4 e5 2. f4 exf4 3. Nf3 Be7
King's Gambit (Declined)	1. e4 e5 2. f4 anything but 2. . . . exf4
King's Gambit (Double Muzio)	1. e4 e5 2. f4 exf4 3. Nf3 g5 4. Bc4 g4 5. O-O gxf3 6. Qxf3 Qf6 7. e5 Qxe5 8. Bxf7+
King's Gambit (Falkbeer Counter Gambit)	1. e4 e5 2. f4 d5

King's Gambit (Fischer's Defense)	1. e4 e5 2. f4 exf4 3. Nf3 d6
King's Gambit (Ghulam Khassim)	1. e4 e5 2. f4 exf4 3. Nf3 g5 4. Bc4 g4 5. d4
King's Gambit (Hanstein Gambit)	1. e4 e5 2. f4 exf4 3. Nf3 g5 4. Bc4 Bg7 5. O-O
King's Gambit (Keene Defense)	1. e4 e5 2. f4 Qh4+ 3. g3 Qe7
King's Gambit (Keres)	1. e4 e5 2. f4 exf4 3. Nc3
King's Gambit (Kieseritzky Gambit)	1. e4 e5 2. f4 exf4 3. Nf3 g5 4. h4 g4 5. Ne5
King's Gambit (King Knight's Gambit)	1. e4 e5 2. f4 exf4 3. Nf3
King's Gambit (King's Bishop Gambit)	1. e4 e5 2. f4 exf4 3. Bc4
King's Gambit (Lesser Bishop's Gambit)	1. e4 e5 2. f4 exf4 3. Be2
King's Gambit (Lopez-Gianutio)	1. e4 e5 2. f4 exf4 3. Bc4 f5
King's Gambit (McDonnell)	1. e4 e5 2. f4 exf4 3. Nf3 g5 4. Bc4 g4 5. Nc3
King's Gambit (Muzio Gambit)	1. e4 e5 2. f4 exf4 3. Nf3 g5 4. Bc4 g4 5. O-O
King's Gambit (Norwalde Variation)	1. e4 e5 2. f4 Qf6
King's Gambit (Pernau)	see King's Gambit (Keres)
King's Gambit (Philidor Gambit)	1. e4 e5 2. f4 exf4 3. Nf3 g5 4. Bc4 Bg7 5. h4 h6 6. d4 d6 7. c3
King's Gambit (Quaade)	1. e4 e5 2. f4 exf4 3. Nf3 g5 4. Nc3
King's Gambit (Rice Gambit)	1. e4 e5 2. f4 exf4 3. Nf3 g5 4. h4 g4 5. Ne5 Nf6 6. Bc4 d5 7. exd5 Bd6 8. O-O
King's Gambit (Rosentreter)	1. e4 e5 2. f4 exf4 3. Nf3 g5 4. d4 g4 5. Bf4
King's Gambit (Salvio)	1. e4 e5 2. f4 exf4 3. Nf3 g5 4. Bc4 g4 5. Ne5
King's Gambit (Sorensen)	1. e4 e5 2. f4 exf4 3. Nf3 g5 4. d4 g4 5. Ne5
King's Gambit (Willemson)	1. e4 e5 2. f4 exf4 3. d4
King's Indian Attack	1. e4, 2. d3, 3. Nbd2, 4. Nf3, 5. g3, 6. Bg2, 7. O-O
King's Indian Defense	1. d4 Nf6 2. c4 g6 3. Nc3 Bg7

King's Indian Defense (Averbakh Variation)	1. d4 Nf6 2. c4 g6 3. Nc3 Bg7 4. e4 d6 5. Be2 O-O 6. Bg5
King's Indian Defense (Classical Variation)	1. d4 Nf6 2. c4 g6 3. Nc3 Bg7 4. e4 d6 5. Nf3 O-O 6. Be2
King's Indian Defense (Fianchetto System)	1. d4 Nf6 2. c4 g6 3. g3 Bg7 4. Bg2 O-O 5. Nc3 d6 6. Nf3
King's Indian Defense (Four Pawns Attack)	1. d4 Nf6 2. c4 g6 3. Nc3 Bg7 4. e4 d6 5. f4
King's Indian Defense (Makogonov Variation)	1. d4 Nf6 2. c4 g6 3. Nc3 Bg7 4. e4 d6 5. h3
King's Indian Defense (Old Indian Defense)	1. d4 Nf6 2. c4 d6
King's Indian Defense (Panno Variation)	1. d4 Nf6 2. c4 g6 3. Nc3 Bg7 4. e4 d6 5. f3 O-O 6. Be3 Nc6
King's Indian Defense (Reversed)	see King's Indian Attack
King's Indian Defense (Robatsch Defense)	see Modern Defense
King's Indian Defense (Sämisch Attack)	1. d4 Nf6 2. c4 g6 3. Nc3 Bg7 4. e4 d6 5. f3
King's Indian Defense (Sämisch-Orthodox Variation)	1. d4 Nf6 2. c4 g6 3. Nc3 Bg7 4. e4 d6 5. f3 O-O 6. Be3 e5
King's Indian Defense (Yugoslav Line)	1. d4 Nf6 2. c4 g6 3. g3 Bg7 4. Bg2 O-O 5. Nc3 d6 6. Nf3 c5
Larsen Attack	1. b3
Latvian Gambit	1. e4 e5 2. Nf3 f5
Latvian Gambit (Corkscrew)	1. e4 e5 2. Nf3 f5 3. Ne5 Nf6 4.Bc4 fxe4 5. Nxf7 Qe7 6. Nxh8 d5
Lemming	1. e4 Na6
Lisitsin Gambit	1. Nf3 f5 2. e4
Mengarini Attack	1. d4 Nf6 2. c4 g6 3. Qc2
Mieses Opening	1. d3
Modern Defense	1. e4 g6
Modern Defense (Pterodactyl)	1. e4 g6 2. d4 Bg7 3. c4 d6 4. Nc3 c5 5. Nf3 Qa5
Modern Defense (Randspringer Variation)	1. e4 g6 2. d4 Bg7 3. c4 d6 4. Nc3 f5
Modern Defense (Rossolimo Variation)	1. e4 g6 2. d4 Bg7 3. c4 d6 4. Nf3 Bg4
Napoleon	1. e4 e5 2. Qf3

Nimzo-Indian Defense	1. d4 Nf6 2. c4 e6 3. Nc3 Bb4
Nimzo-Indian Defense (Classical Variation)	1. d4 Nf6 2. c4 e6 3. Nc3 Bb4 4. Qc2
Nimzo-Indian Defense (Dutch)	see Dutch Defense (Nimzo-Indian)
Nimzo-Indian Defense (Fischer Variation)	1. d4 Nf6 2. c4 e6 3. Nc3 Bb4 4. e3 b6
Nimzo-Indian Defense (Gligoric Variation)	1. d4 Nf6 2. c4 e6 3. Nc3 Bb4 4. e3 O-O 5. Bd3 d5 6. Nf3 c5 7. O-O
Nimzo-Indian Defense (Hübner Variation)	1. d4 Nf6 2. c4 e6 3. Nc3 Bb4 4. e3 c5 5. Bd3 Nc6 6. Nf3 Bxc3 +
Nimzo-Indian Defense (Leningrad Variation)	1. d4 Nf6 2. c4 e6 3. Nc3 Bb4 4. Bg5
Nimzo-Indian Defense (Mikenas Attack)	1. d4 Nf6 2. c4 e6 3. Nc3 Bb4 4. Qd3
Nimzo-Indian Defense (Milner-Barry Variation)	1. d4 Nf6 2. c4 e6 3. Nc3 Bb4 4. Qc2 Nc6
Nimzo-Indian Defense (Rubinstein Variation)	1. d4 Nf6 2. c4 e6 3. Nc3 Bb4 4. e3
Nimzo-Indian Defense (Sämisch Variation)	1. d4 Nf6 2. c4 e6 3. Nc3 Bb4 4. a3
Nimzo-Indian Defense (Spielmann Variation)	1. d4 Nf6 2. c4 e6 3. Nc3 Bb4 4. Qb3
Nimzovich Defense	1. e4 Nc6
Nimzovich Defense (Marshall Gambit)	1. e4 Nc6 2. d4 d5 3. exd5 Qxd5 4. Nc3
Orangutan	see Sokolsky Opening
Owen Defense	1. e4 b6
Paris Opening	1. Nh3
Petrov's Defense	1. e4 e5 2. Nf3 Nf6
Petrov's Defense (Cochrane Gambit)	1. e4 e5 2. Nf3 Nf6 3. Nxe5 d6 4. Nxf7
Philidor's Defense	1. e4 e5 2. Nf3 d6
Philidor's Defense (Locock)	1. e4 e5 2. Nf3 d6 3. d4 Nf6 4. Ng5 h6 5. Nxf7
Philidor's Defense (Lopez Counter Gambit)	1. e4 e5 2. Nf3 d6 3. Bc4 f5
Pirc Defense	1. e4 d6
Pirc Defense (Austrian Attack)	1. e4 d6 2. d4 Nf6 3. Nc3 g6 4. f4

Pirc Defense (Byrne Variation)	1. e4 d6 2. d4 Nf6 3. Nc3 g6 4. Bg5
Pirc Defense (Classical System)	1. e4 d6 2. d4 Nf6 3. Nc3 g6 4. Nf3 Bg7
Pirc Defense (Fianchetto Variation)	1. e4 d6 2. d4 Nf6 3. Nc3 g6 4. g3
Pirc Defense (Reversed)	1. Nf3 d5 2. g3 Nc6 3. Bg2 e5 4. d3
Polish Attack	see Sokolsky Opening
Polish Defense	1. d4 b5
Polish Gambit	1. d4 d5 2. e4 dxe4 3. Nc3 Bf6 4. Bg5
Ponziani Opening	1. e4 e5 2. Nf3 Nc6 3. c3
Queen's Bishop Attack	1. d4 d5 2. Bg5
Queen's Gambit	1. d4 d5 2. c4
Queen's Gambit (Abrahams-Noteboom Variation)	1. d4 d5 2. c4 c6 3. Nc3 e6 4. Nf3 dxc4 5. a4 Bb4 6. e3 b5 7. Bd2 a5
Queen's Gambit (Accepted)	1. d4 d5 2. c4 dxc4
Queen's Gambit (Albin Counter Gambit)	1. d4 d5 2. c4 e5
Queen's Gambit (Anti-Meran Variation)	1. d4 d5 2. c4 c6 3. Nf3 Nf6 4. Nc3 e6 5. Bg5
Queen's Gambit (Cambridge Springs Defense)	1. d4 d5 2. c4 e6 3. Nc3 Nf6 4. Bg5 Nbd7 5. e3 c6 6. Nf3 Qa5
Queen's Gambit (Chigorin's Defense)	1. d4 d5 2. c4 Nc6
Queen's Gambit (Classical Variation)	1. d4 d5 2. c4 e6 3. Nc3 Nf6 4. Nf3 Be7 5. Bf4
Queen's Gambit (Declined)	1. d4 d5 2. c4 anything but 2. . . . dxc4
Queen's Gambit (Dutch Variation)	1. d4 d5 2. c4 e6 3. Nc3 Nf6 4. Bg5 c5 5. cxd5 cxd4
Queen's Gambit (Exchange Variation)	1. d4 d5 2. c4 e6 3. Nc3 Nf6 4. cxd5 exd5
Queen's Gambit (Janowski Variation)	1. d4 d5 2. c4 e6 3. Nc3 a6
Queen's Gambit (Lasker's Defense)	1. d4 d5 2. c4 e6 3. Nc3 Nf6 4. Bg5 Be7 5. e3 O-O 6. Nf3 h6 7. Bh4 Ne4
Queen's Gambit (Manhattan Variation)	1. d4 d5 2. c4 e6 3. Nc3 Nf6 4. Bg5 Nbd7 5. e3 Bb4

Queen's Gambit (Marshall Gambit)	1. d4 d5 2. c4 e6 3. Nc3 c5 4. cxd5 exd5 5. e4
Queen's Gambit (Marshall Variation)	1. d4 d5 2. c4 Nf6
Queen's Gambit (Meran Variation)	1. d4 d5 2. c4 c6 3. Nf3 Nf6 4. Nc3 e6 5. e3 Nbd7 6. Bd3 dxc4
Queen's Gambit (Orthodox Defense)	1. d4 d5 2. c4 e6 3. Nc3 Nf6 4. Bg5 Be7 5. e3 O-O 6. Nf3 Nbd7
Queen's Gambit (Peruvian)	1. d4 d5 2. c4 e6 3. Nc3 Nf6 4. Bg5 c5
Queen's Gambit (Petrosian Variation)	1. d4 d5 2. c4 e6 3. Nc3 Nf6 4. Bg5 Be7 5. e3 O-O 6. Nf3 h6 7. Bxf6
Queen's Gambit (Ragozin System)	1. d4 d5 2. c4 e6 3. Nc3 Nf6 4. Nf3 Bb4
Queen's Gambit (Reynolds Variation)	1. d4 d5 2. c4 c6 3. Nf3 Nf6 4. Nc3 e6 5. e3 Nbd7 6. Bd3 dxc4 7. Bxc4 b5 8. Bd3 a6 9. e4 c5 10. d5
Queen's Gambit (Romih Variation)	1. d4 d5 2. c4 c6 3. Nf3 Nf6 4. Nc3 e6 5. e3 Nbd7 6. Bd3 Bb4
Queen's Gambit (Sahovic Defense)	1. d5 d5 2. c4 Bf5
Queen's Gambit (Semi-Slav Defense)	1. d4 d5 2. c4 c6 3. Nf3 Nf6 4. Nc3 e6
Queen's Gambit (Semi-Tarrasch Defense)	1. d4 d5 2. c4 e6 3. Nc3 Nf6 4. Nf3 c5
Queen's Gambit (Slav Defense)	1. d4 d5 2. c4 c6
Queen's Gambit (Swedish Variation)	1. d4 d5 2. c4 e6 3. Nc3 c5 4. cxd5 exd5 5. Nf3 Nc6 6. g3 c4
Queen's Gambit (Tarrasch Defense)	1. d4 d5 2. c4 e6 3. Nc3 c5
Queen's Gambit (Tarrasch-Rubinstein Variation)	1. d4 d5 2. c4 c6 3. Nc3 c5 4. cxd5 exd5 5. Nf3 Nc6 6. g3
Queen's Gambit (Tartakower Variation)	1. d4 d5 2. c4 e6 3. Nc3 Nf6 4. Bg5 Be7 5. e3 O-O 6. Nf3 h6 7. Bh4 b6
Queen's Gambit (Vienna Variation)	1. d4 d5 2. c4 e6 3. Nf3 Nf6 4. Bg5 Bb4+
Queen's Gambit (von Hennig-Schara Gambit)	1. d4 d5 2. c4 e6 3. Nc3 c5 4. cxd5 cxd4
Queen's Gambit (Winawer Counter Gambit)	1. d4 d5 2. c4 c6 3. Nc3 e5

Queen's Indian Defense	1. d4 Nf6 2. c4 e6 3. Nf3 b6
Queen's Indian Defense (Petrosian System)	1. d4 Nf6 2. c4 e6 3. Nf3 b6 4. a3
Queen's Knight Defense	1. d4 Nc6 2. c4
Relfsson Gambit	1. e4 e5 2. Nf3 Nc6 3. d4 exd4 4. Bb5
Reti Opening	1. Nf3 d5
Reti Opening (Barcza System)	1. Nf3 d5 2. g3
Reti Opening (Benoni Reversed)	1. Nf3 d5 2. c4 d4
Reti Opening (Gambit Accepted)	1. Nf3 d5 2. c4 dxc4
Reti Opening (Lasker System)	1. Nf3 d5 2. c4 c6 3. b3 Nf6 4. g3 Bf5
Reti Opening (Neo-Catalan)	1. Nf3 d5 2. c4 e6 3. g3
Reti Opening (Polonaise)	1. Nf3 d5 2. c4 d4 3. b4
Richter-Veresov Attack	1. d4 d5 2. Nc3
Russian Game	see Petrov's Defense
Ruth-Trompowsky Attack	1. d4 Nf6 2. Bg5
Ruy Lopez	1. e4 e5 2. Nf3 Nc6 3. Bb5
Ruy Lopez (Alapin Variation)	1. e4 e5 2. Nf3 Nc6 3. Bb5 Bb4
Ruy Lopez (Berlin Defense)	1. e4 e5 2. Nf3 Nc6 3. Bb5 Nf6
Ruy Lopez (Bird's Defense)	1. e4 e5 2. Nf3 Nc6 3. Bb5 Nd4
Ruy Lopez (Classical Defense)	1. e4 e5 2. Nf3 Nc6 3. Bb5 Bc5
Ruy Lopez (Closed Defense)	1. e4 e5 2. Nf3 Nc6 3. Bb5 a6 4. Ba4 Nf6 5. O-O Be7
Ruy Lopez (Closed-Breyer Variation)	1. e4 e5 2. Nf3 Nc6 3. Bb5 a6 4. Ba4 Nf6 5. O-O Be7 6. Re1 b5 7. Bb3 d6 8. c3 O-O 9. h3 Nb8
Ruy Lopez (Closed-Chigorin Variation)	1. e4 e5 2. Nf3 Nc6 3. Bb5 a6 4. Ba4 Nf6 5. O-O Be7 6. Re1 b5 7. Bb3 d6 8. c3 O-O 9. h3 Na5
Ruy Lopez (Closed-Smyslov Variation)	1. e4 e5 2. Nf3 Nc6 3. Bb5 a6 4. Ba4 Nf6 5. O-O Be7 6. Re1 b5 7. Bb3 d6 8. c3 O-O 9. h3 h6
Ruy Lopez (Closed-Zaitsev)	1. e4 e5 2. Nf3 Nc6 3. Bb5 a6 4. Ba4 Nf6 5. O-O Be7 6. Re1 b5 7. Bb3 d6 8. c3 O-O 9. h3 Bb7
Ruy Lopez (Cordel Defense)	see Ruy Lopez (Classical)

Ruy Lopez Lopez (Cozio Defense)	1. e4 e5 2. Nf3 Nc6 3. Bb5 Nge7
Ruy Lopez (Dilworth Attack)	1. e4 e5 2. Nf3 Nc6 3. Bb5 a6 4. Ba4 Nf6 5. O-O Nxe4 6. d4 b5 7. Bb3 d5 8. dxe5 Be6 9. c3 Bc5 10. Nbd2 O-O 11. Bc2 Nxf2
Ruy Lopez (Exchange Variation)	1. e4 e5 2. Nf3 Nc6 3. Bb5 a6 4. Bxc6
Ruy Lopez (Jaenisch Gambit)	see Ruy Lopez (Schliemann)
Ruy Lopez (Marshall Attack)	1. e4 e5 2. Nf3 Nc6 3. Bb5 a6 4. Ba4 Nf6 5. O-O Be7 6. Re1 b5 7. Bb3 O-O 8. c3 d5
Ruy Lopez (Modern Steinitz Defense)	1. e4 e5 2. Nf3 Nc6 3. Bb5 a6 4. Ba4 d6
Ruy Lopez (Open Defense)	1. e4 e5 2. Nf3 Nc6 3. Bb5 a6 4. Ba4 Nf6 5. O-O Nxe4
Ruy Lopez (Open Defense-Harksen)	1. e4 e5 2. Nf3 Nc6 3. Bb5 a6 4. Ba4 Nf6 5. O-O Nxe4 6. d4 b5 7. Bb3 d5 8. c4
Ruy Lopez (Schliemann Gambit)	1. e4 e5 2. Nf3 Nc6 3. Bb5 f5
Ruy Lopez (Siesta Variation)	1. e4 e5 2. Nf3 Nc6 3. Bb5 a6 4. Ba4 d6 5. c3 f5
Ruy Lopez (Steinitz Defense)	1. e4 e5 2. Nf3 Nc6 3. Bb5 d6
Ruy Lopez (Vinogradov)	1. e4 e5 2. Nf3 Nc6 3. Bb5 Qe7
Ruy Lopez (Worrall Attack)	1. e4 e5 2. Nf3 Nc6 3. Bb5 a6 4. Ba4 Nf6 5. O-O Be7 6. Qe2
Santasiere's Folly	1. Nf3 d5 2. b4
Saragossa Opening	1. c3
Scotch Game	1. e4 e5 2. Nf3 Nc6 3. d4
Scotch Game (Goring Gambit)	1. e4 e5 2. Nf3 Nc6 3. d4 exd4 4. c3
Scotch Game (Relfsson)	1. e4 e5 2. Nf3 Nc6 3. d4 exd4 4. Bb5
Scotch Game (Scotch Gambit)	1. e4 e5 2. Nf3 Nc6 3. d4 exd4 4. Bc4
Seirawan Attack	1. d4 Nf6 2. c4 e6 3. Bg5
Sicilian Defense	1. e4 c5
Sicilian Defense (Action Extension)	1. e4 c5 2. Nf3 g6 3. c4 Bh6
Sicilian Defense (Boleslavsky Variation)	1. e4 c5 2. Nf3 Nc6 3. d4 cxd4 4. Nxd4 Nf6 5. Nc3 d6 6. Be2 e5
Sicilian Defense (Chameleon)	1. e4 c5 2. Ne2, 3) Nbc3 or 2) Nc3, 3) Nge2

Sicilian Defense (Closed Variation)	1. e4 c5 2. Nc3
Sicilian Defense (Dragon Variation)	1. e4 c5 2. Nf3 d6 3. d4 cxd4 4. Nxd4 Nf6 5. Nc3 g6
Sicilian Defense (Dragon Variation-Zollner)	1. e4 c5 2. Nf3 d6 3. d4 cxd4 4. Nxd4 Nf6 5. Nc3 g6 6. Be2 Bg7 7. O-O O-O 8. Be3 Nc6 9. f4 Qb6 10. e5
Sicilian Defense (Dragon-Accelerated)	1. e4 c5 2. Nf3 Nc6 3. d4 cxd4 4. Nxd4 g6
Sicilian Defense (Dragon-Classical)	1. e4 c5 2. Nf3 d6 3. d4 cxd4 4. Nxd4 Nf6 5. Nc3 g6 6. Be2
Sicilian Defense (f4 Attack)	1. e4 c5 2. f4
Sicilian Defense (Four Knights Variation)	1. e4 c5 2. Nf3 e6 3. d4 cxd4 4. Nxd4 Nf6 5. Nc3 Nc6
Sicilian Defense (Goteborg Variation)	1. e4 c5 2. Nf3 d6 3. d4 cxd4 4. Nxd4 Nf6 5. Nc3 a6 6. Bg5 e6 7. f4 Be7 8. Qf3 h6 9. Bh4 g5
Sicilian Defense (Kan Variation)	see Sicilian Defense (Paulsen)
Sicilian Defense (Keres Attack)	1. e4 c5 2. Nf3 e6 3. d4 cxd4 4. Nxd4 Nf6 5. Nc3 d6 6. g4
Sicilian Defense (Larsen Grand Prix)	see Sicilian Defense (f4 Attack)
Sicilian Defense (Larsen Variation)	1. e4 c5 2. Nf3 Nc6 3. d4 cxd4 4. Nxd4 Nf6 5. Nc3 d6 6. Bg5 Bd7
Sicilian Defense (Lasker-Pelikan Variation)	see Sicilian Defense (Sveshnikov)
Sicilian Defense (Levenfish Variation)	1. e4 c5 2. Nf3 d6 3. d4 cxd4 4. Nxd4 Nf6 5. Nc3 g6 6. f4
Sicilian Defense (Lowenthal Variation)	1. e4 c5 2. Nf3 Nc6 3. d4 cxd4 4. Nxd4 e5
Sicilian Defense (Maróczy Bind)	1. e4 c5 2. Nf3 Nc6 3. d4 cxd4 4. Nxd4 g6 5. c4
Sicilian Defense (Morra Gambit)	1. e4 c5 2. d4 cxd4 3. c3
Sicilian Defense (Morra Gambit-Accepted)	1. e4 c5 2. d4 cxd4 3. c3 dxc3
Sicilian Defense (Morra Gambit-Declined)	1. e4 c5 2. d4 cxd4 3. c3 anything but 3) . . . dxc3
Sicilian Defense (Najdorf Variation)	1. e4 c5 2. Nf3 d6 3. d4 cxd4 4. Nxd4 Nf6 5. Nc3 a6

Sicilian Defense (Najdorf Variation-poisoned pawn)	1. e4 c5 2. Nf3 d6 3. d4 cxd4 4. Nxd4 Nf6 5. Nc3 a6 6. Bg5 e6 7. f4 Qb6 8. Qd2 Qxb2
Sicilian Defense (Neo-Sveshnikov Variation)	1. e4 c5 2. Nf3 Nc6 3. d4 cxd4 4. Nxd4 e5 5. Ndb5 db
Sicilian Defense (Paulsen Variation)	1. e4 c5 2. Nf3 e6 3. d4 cxd4 4. Nxd4 a6
Sicilian Defense (Polugaevsky Variation)	1. e4 c5 2. Nf3 d6 3. d4 cxd4 4. Nxd4 Nf6 5. Nc3 a6 6. Bg5 e6 7. f4 b5
Sicilian Defense (Quinteros Variation)	1. e4 c5 2. Nf3 Qc7
Sicilian Defense (Reversed)	1. c4 e5
Sicilian Defense (Richter-Rauser Variation)	1. e4 c5 2. Nf3 Nc6 3. d4 cxd4 4. Nxd4 Nf6 5. Nc3 d6 6. Bg5
Sicilian Defense (Rossolimo Attack)	1. e4 c5 2. Nf3 Nc6 3. Bb5
Sicilian Defense (Scheveningen Variation)	1. e4 c5 2. Nf3 e6 3. d4 cxd4 4. Nxd4 Nf6 5. Nc3 d6 6. Be2 Nc6
Sicilian Defense (Slow)	1. e4 c5 2. Bc2
Sicilian Defense (Smith-Morra Gambit)	see Sicilian Defense (Morra Gambit)
Sicilian Defense (Snyder Variation)	1. e4 c5 2. b3
Sicilian Defense (Sozin)	1. e4 c5 2. Nf3 Nc6 3. d4 cxd4 4. Nxd4 Nf6 5. Nc3 d6 6. Bc4
Sicilian Defense (Stiletto Variation)	1. e4 c5 2. Nf3 Qa5
Sicilian Defense (Sveshnikov Variation)	1. e4 c5 2. Nf3 Nc6 3. d4 cxd4 4. Nxd4 Nf6 5. Nc3 e5
Sicilian Defense (Taimanov Variation)	1. e4 c5 2. Nf3 e6 3. d4 cxd4 4. Nxd4 Nc6
Sicilian Defense (Velimirovic Attack)	1. e4 c5 2. Nf3 Nc6 3. d4 cxd4 4. Nxd4 Nf6 5. Nc3 d6 6. Bc4 e6 7. Be3 Be7 8. Qe2
Sicilian Defense (Wing Gambit)	1. e4 c5 2. b4
Sicilian Defense (Wing Gambit-Marshall Variation)	1. e4 c5 2. b4 cxb4 3. a3
Sicilian Defense (Yugoslav Attack)	1. e4 c5 2. Nf3 d6 3. d4 cxd4 4. Nxd4 Nf6 5. Nc3 g6 6. Be3 Bg7 7. f3

Sokolsky Opening	1. b4
Spanish	see Ruy Lopez
Spike	1. g4
St. George Defense	1. e4 a6 2. d4 b5
Tayler Opening	1. e4 e5 2. Nf3 Nc6 3. Be2
Tennison Gambit	see Abonyi Gambit
Three Knights Game	1. e4 e5 2. Nf3 Nc6 3. Nc3
Torre Attack	1. d4 Nf6 2. Nf3 e6 3. Bg5
Trompowsky	1. d4 Nf6 2. Bg5
Two Knights Defense	1 e4 e5 2. Nf3 Nc6 3. Bc4 Nf6
Two Knights Defense (Canal Variation)	1. e4 e5 2. Nf3 Nc6 3. Bc4 Nf6 4. d4 exd4 5. O-O Nxe4 6. Re1 d5 7. Nc3
Two Knights Defense (Fried Liver Attack)	1. e4 e5 2. Nf3 Nc6 3. Bc4 Nf6 4. Ng5 d5 5. exd5 Nxd5 6. Nxf7
Two Knights Defense (Fritz Variation)	1. e4 e5 2. Nf3 Nc6 3. Bc4 Nf6 4. Ng5 d5 5. exd5 Nd4
Two Knights Defense (Max Lange Attack)	1. e4 d5 2. Nf3 Nc6 3. Bc4 Nf6 4. d4 exd4 5. O-O Bc5 6. e5
Two Knights Defense (Pinkus Variation)	1. e4 e5 2. Nf3 Nc6 3. Bc4 Nf6 4. Ng5 d5 5. exd5 Nxd5 6. d4 Bb4 +
Two Knights Defense (Traxler Variation)	see Two Knights Defense (Wilkes-Barre Variation)
Two Knights Defense (Ulvestad Variation)	1. e4 e5 2. Nf3 Nc6 3. Bc4 Nf6 4. Ng5 d5 5. exd5 b5
Two Knights Defense (Wilkes-Barre Variation)	1. e4 e5 2. Nf3 Nc6 3. Bc4 Nf6 4. Ng5 Bc5
Two Knights Defense (Lolli)	1. e4 e5 2. Nf3 Nc6 3. Bc4 Nf6 4. Ng5 d5 5. exd5 Nxd5 6. d4
Van't Kruij's Opening	1. e3
Venezolana	d3, Nc3, g3
Vienna Game	1. e4 e5 2. Nc3
Vienna Game (Frankenstein-Dracula)	1. e4 e5 2. Nc3 Nf6 3. Bc4 Nxe4 4. Qh5 Nd 5. Bd3 Nc6 6. Nb5 g6 7. Qf3 f5 8. Qd5 Qe7 9. Nxc7 + Kd8 10. Nxa8
Vienna Game (Fyfe)	1. e4 e5 2. Nc3 Nc6 3. d4
Vienna Game (Hamppe-Allgaier Gambit)	1. e4 e5 2. Nc3 Nc6 3. f4 exf4 4. Nf3 g5 5. h4 g4 6. Ng5
Vienna Game (Hamppe-Muzio)	1. e4 e5 2. Nc3 Nc6 3. f4 exf4 4. Nf3 g5 5. Bc4 g4 6. O-O

Vienna Game (Pierce Gambit)	1. e4 e5 2. Nc3 Nc6 3. f4 exf4 4. Nf3 g5 5. d4
Vienna Game (Steinitz Gambit)	1. e4 e5 2. Nc3 Nc6 3. f4 exf4 4. d4 Qh4+ 5. Ke2
Vienna Game (Vienna Gambit)	1. e4 e5 2. Nc3 Nf6 3. f4
Vulture	1. d4 c5 2. d5 Nf6 3. c4 Ne4
Wade Defense	1. Nf3 d6
Woozle	1. d4 c5 2. d5 Nf6 3. Nc3 Qa5

C. TACTICS

∎

ABSOLUTE PIN
ACTIVATE
ALTERNATION
AMBUSH
ANNIHILATION
ARITHMETIC
ATTACK
ATTRACTION
BIFFING THE BISHOP
BLUNDER
BREAKING THE PIN
BREAKTHROUGH
BREAKTHROUGH COMBINATION
BRIDGE
BUILDING A BRIDGE
BUST UP
CALCULATION
CALCULATION OF VARIATIONS
CHEAPO
CHECK
CLEARANCE
COMBINATION
CORRAL
CORRALLING A KNIGHT
COUNTING
CROSS-CHECK
CROSS-PIN
DECOY
DEFENSE
DEFLECTION
DESPERADO
DIRECT ATTACK
DIRECT PROTECTION
DISCOVERED ATTACK
DISCOVERED CHECK
DISCOVERY
DOMINATION
DOUBLE ATTACK
DOUBLE CHECK
DOUBLE THREAT
DRIVING BACK

DRIVING OFF
DRIVING ON
EN PRISE
ENVELOPING ATTACK
ENVELOPING MANEUVER
EVEN EXCHANGE
EVEN TRADE
EXCHANGE
EXCHANGE SACRIFICE
FAMILY CHECK
FAMILY FORK
FAST MOVE
FEINT
FOR FREE
FOR NOTHING
FORCE
FORCING
FORCING MOVE
FORK
FORKING CHECK
FORK TRICK
FRONTIER ATTACK
GAIN A MOVE
GAIN A TEMPO
GRANDE COMBINAISON
HANGING
HUNG A PAWN
HUNG MATE
HURDLE
IN-BETWEEN MOVE
INDIRECT
INDIRECT DEFENSE
INDIRECT THREAT
INTERFERENCE
INTERPOSE
INTERPOSITION
JETTISON
KICK
KNIGHT CORRAL
KNIGHT FORK
LIQUIDATE

LUFT
MAKE LUFT
MYSTERIOUS ROOK MOVE
OBSTRUCT
OBSTRUCTION
OCCUPATION
ONE-MOVER
OPPOSITION
OUTFLANKING
OVERLOAD
OVERLOADED
OVERWORKED PIECE
PARRY A CHECK
PAWN FORK
PAWN RACE
PERPETUAL CHECK
PETITE COMBINAISON
PILING ON
PIN
PIN BREAKING
PIN MATE
PIN OVERLOAD
POINTLESS CHECK
PREVENTING CASTLING
PREVENTIVE SACRIFICE
PROMOTION
PROTECTION
PSEUDO SACRIFICE
PUTTING THE QUESTION TO THE
  BISHOP
QUEEN FORK
QUEENING
QUEENING A PAWN
QUIET MOVE
REAR ATTACK
RECAPTURE
REFUTATION
REFUTE
RELATIVE PIN
REMOVING THE DEFENDER
REMOVING THE GUARD
REVERSE PIN
ROOK LIFT
ROYAL FORK
SAVING
SEESAW
SELF-BLOCK
SELF-PIN
SETUP CHECK
SHAM SACRIFICE
SHISH KEBAB ATTACK

SHOT
SHUT-OFF
SIMPLIFICATION
SIMPLIFY
SKEWER
SKEWER CHECK
SLOW MOVE
SMOTHERED MATE
SOUND
SPECULATIVE
SPITE CHECK
SQUARE VACATION
SQUEEZE
STRATAGEM
SUCKER PUNCH
SWIMMING
SWINDLE
TACTICAL FINESSE
TACTICIAN
TACTICS
TAKE
TAKE BACK
TEMPO MOVE
TEMPORARY SACRIFICE
THREAT
TIMING
TRADE
TRANSPOSE
TRANSPOSITION
TRAP
TRAPPING
TRAPPY MOVE
UNBLOCK
UNDERMINING
UNPIN
UNSOUND
USELESS CHECK
VACATE
VACATION
WAITING MOVE
WALLING IN
WASTE A MOVE
WIN THE EXCHANGE
WINDMILL
WINDMILL ATTACK
WITH CHECK
X-RAY
X-RAY ATTACK
X-RAY DEFENSE
ZUGZWANG
ZWISCHENZUG

D. ADVICE TECHNIQUES

■

ACCUMULATION OF ADVANTAGES
AGREED DRAW
AIMLESS DEVELOPMENT
ALTERNATION
AMAUROSIS SCACCHISTICA
ANALYSIS
ANALYTIC METHOD
ANALYZE
ANNOUNCED MATE
ANTI-POSITIONAL MOVE
ARITHMETIC
ASYMMETRICAL
ASYMMETRY
ATTACK AT THE BASE OF THE PAWN
   CHAIN
BAD CHECK
BEHIND A PASSED PAWN
BEST BY TEST
CALCULATION
CALCULATION OF VARIATIONS
CANDIDATE MOVE
CAPABLANCA'S RULE
CASTLE BY HAND
CASTLE EARLY
CENTRALIZATION
CLASSICAL
CLASSICAL PAWN CENTER
COFFEEHOUSE CHESS
COMPENSATION
COMPLICATE
COMPLICATIONS
CONNECTING THE ROOKS
CONSOLIDATE
CONSOLIDATION
COUNTERATTACK
COUNTERCHANCES
COUNTERGAMBIT
COUNTERPLAY
COUNTING

DARK-SQUARE GAME
DERIVATIVE
DEVELOP
DEVELOP TOWARD THE CENTER
DEVELOPMENT
DOUBLING
ERROR
EVALUATION
FREEING MANEUVER
FREEING MOVE
HOME ANALYSIS
HYPERMODERN
ILLEGAL MOVE
INITIATIVE
INNOVATIVE
INTUITIVE PLAYER
JUDGMENT
KIBITZ
KILLER INSTINCT
KNIGHT ON THE RIM IS DIM
KNIGHTS BEFORE BISHOPS
LIGHT-SQUARE GAME
LIQUIDATION
MAKE LUFT
MANEUVER
METHOD
METHODICAL
OPENING REPERTOIRE
OVEREXTENSION
OVERPROTECTION
PASSED PAWNS MUST BE PUSHED
PATTERN RECOGNITION
PAWN-GRABBING
PAWN-SNATCHING
PLANNING
PLAY THE BOARD, NOT THE MAN
POINTLESS CHECK
PREMATURE
PREPARED VARIATION

PROPHYLAXIS
REVERSING THE MOVE ORDER
ROMANTIC
ROOKS BELONG BEHIND PASSED
  PAWNS
ROOKS BELONG ON OPEN FILES
SCHOOL OF CHESS
SIMPLIFICATION
SIMPLIFY
SOUND
SPECULATIVE
SPITE CHECK
STYLE
STYLISTIC
TAKE THE OPPOSITION
TAKE TOWARDS THE CENTER

TECHNIQUE
TIME PRESSURE
TIME TROUBLE
TIMING
TRANSPOSE
TRIPLE
UNDERDEVELOPED
UNDEVELOPED
UNNECESSARY PAWN MOVES
UNSOUND
USELESS CHECK
VIOLATION OF PRINCIPLE
VISUALIZATION
WASTING TIME
ZEITNOT

E. PEOPLE

■

ANALYST
ANT
ARBITER
BEGINNER
BOOK PLAYER
CHESSMASTER
CHILD PRODIGY
DUFFER
ELO RATING
FISH
FISHCAKE
GAMBITEER
GM
GRANDMASTER
INTERNATIONAL GRANDMASTER
INTERNATIONAL MASTER
INTUITIVE PLAYER
KIBITZER
KILLER INSTINCT
MASTER
METHODICAL
NATIONAL MASTER

NN
PATZER
PAWN AND MOVE
PAWN AND TWO MOVES
ODDS
HANDICAP
PAWN-GRABBER
PAWN-SNATCHER
RABBIT
RANK BEGINNER
RATING
ROMANTIC
SECOND
SITZFLEISCH
STYLE
THEORETICIAN
TITLE
TOURNAMENT DIRECTOR
WOODPUSHER
WOODSHIFTER
WOODTHUMPER

F. GEOGRAPHY

■

BACK RANK
BACK ROW
BASIC CENTER
BISHOP-PAWN
BLACK SQUARES
CAMP
CENTER
CENTRAL
CENTRAL ZONE
CENTRALIZE
CHESSBOARD
COLUMN
COORDINATE GRID
DANGEROUS DIAGONAL
DARK SQUARES
DIAGONAL
DOWN
EDGE
EIGHTH RANK
ENLARGED CENTER
ESCAPE SQUARE
FIANCHETTO
FILE
FLANK
FLANKING A BISHOP
FLIGHT SQUARE
FORWARD
FRONTIER
FRONTIER LINE
HOLE
HORIZONTAL ROW
IN FRONT
KB-FILE
KING-BISHOP FILE
KING FILE
KING-KNIGHT FILE
KING-ROOK FILE
KING'S WING

KINGSIDE
KN-FILE
LIGHT ON THE RIGHT RULE
LINE
LONG DIAGONAL
LONG SIDE
OPEN FILE
PROMOTION SQUARE
QUADRANGLE
QUADRANT
QUEEN-BISHOP FILE
QUEEN FILE
QUEEN-KNIGHT FILE
QUEEN ON ITS OWN COLOR
QUEEN-ROOK FILE
QUEEN'S WING
QUEENING FILE
QUEENING SQUARE
QUEENSIDE
RANK
REMOTE CORNER
RIGHT CORNER
RIGHT TRIANGLE CHECK
RIGHT TRIANGLE MATE
ROOK FILE
SEVENTH
SEVENTH RANK
SHORT SIDE
SQUARE
TERRITORY
UP
UP THE BOARD
VERTICAL LINE
VERTICAL ROW
WHITE SQUARES
WING
WRONG CORNER

G. GAME VARIATIONS

■

ALLIES
ANALYSIS
BLINDFOLD CHESS
BLITZ
BUGHOUSE
CASUAL GAME
CHATURANGA
CHESS BY MAIL
CLOCK GAME
COFFEEHOUSE CHESS
COMPOSED PROBLEM
COMPOSITION
CONDITIONAL PROBLEM
CONSULTATION GAME
CORRESPONDENCE CHESS
EIGHT QUEENS PROBLEM
EXHIBITION
EXHIBITION GAME
EXHIBITION MATCH
FIVE-MINUTE CHESS
FIVE-MINUTE GAME
GAME THEORY
GIVE ODDS
HANDICAP
HELPMATE
IN TANDEM
INSANITY CHESS
KNIGHT'S TOUR
KRIEGSPIEL
LIGHTNING CHESS
LIVING CHESS
MATCH
MOVE ON MOVE
NORMAL CHESS
ODDS
OFFHAND GAMES
ONE-MOVER
OPEN TOURNAMENT
OVER THE BOARD

PAWN AND MOVE
PAWN AND TWO MOVES
PERFECT INFORMATION
POST MORTEM
POSTAL GAME
PRAXIS
PROBLEM
PUZZLE
RACE GAME
RAPID CHESS
RAPID TRANSIT CHESS
RETROGRADE ANALYSIS
ROUND ROBIN
SANS VOIR
SELF-MATE
SHATRANJ
SHOGI
SIMUL
SIMULTANEOUS
SIMULTANEOUS BLINDFOLD
  EXHIBITION
SIMULTANEOUS DISPLAY
SIMULTANEOUS EXHIBITION
SKITTLES
STUDY
SUI-MATE
SWISS SYSTEM
TANDEM
TANDEM PUT-BACK
TASK
TEN-SECOND CHESS
THREE-DIMENSIONAL CHESS
THREE-MOVER
TOURNAMENT
TWO-MOVE MATE
TWO-MOVER
WAR GAME
WHITE TO PLAY AND WIN
ZERO-SUM GAME

H. PATTERNS

■

ALIGNED BISHOPS
ANASTASIA'S MATE
ARABIAN MATE
BACK-RANK MATE
BACK-ROW MATE
BATTERY
BLIND SWINE MATE
BODEN'S MATE
CENTURINI'S POSITION
CIRCUIT
CLASSIC BISHOP SACRIFICE
CONNECTED
CONNECTING THE ROOKS
CORRIDOR MATE
DOUBLE
DOUBLE-BISHOP SACRIFICE
DOUBLE FIANCHETTO
DOUBLE-ROOK SACRIFICE
DOUBLED ROOKS
DOUBLING
EPAULET MATE
FEGATELLO ATTACK
FOOL'S MATE
FRIED LIVER ATTACK

GRECO'S MATE
GUERIDON MATE
HORRWITZ BISHOPS
IMMORTAL GAME
KING HUNT
LEGAL'S MATE
LEGAL'S SACRIFICE
LUCENA'S POSITION
NOAH'S ARK TRAP
PHILIDOR'S DRAW
PHILIDOR'S LEGACY
PHILIDOR'S POSITION
RAKING BISHOPS
SAAVEDRA'S POSITION
SCHOLAR'S MATE
SUPPORT MATE
SWALLOW'S TAIL MATE
SZEN POSITION
TARRASCH TRAP
TRÉBUCHET
TRIANGULATION
TRIPLE
TURNING MANEUVER
TWO-BISHOP SACRIFICE

I. ADMINISTRATION AND PARAPHENALIA

∎

ADMINISTRATION

ADJOURN
ADJOURNED POSITION
ADJOURNMENT
ADJUDICATE
ADJUDICATION
ALGEBRAIC NOTATION
ARBITER
BEAUTY PRIZE
BRILLIANCY PRIZE
BYE
CLOCK GAME
COMPUTER NOTATION
COORDINATE NOTATION
CROSSTABLE
DESCRIPTIVE NOTATION
ELO RATING
FIDE
FIDE LAWS OF CHESS
FORFEIT
LAWS OF CHESS
LEGAL
MOVES AND RULES
NOTATION
PAIRING
RATING
SCORING
SEALED MOVE
TD
TIME CONTROL
TIME LIMIT
TITLE
TOURNAMENT DIRECTOR
UNITED STATES CHESS FEDERATION
USCF

CHESS PARAPHENALIA

ANNOTATED GAME
ANNOTATION
BLACK PIECES
BOARD
CHESSBOARD
CHESS CLOCK
CHESSMEN
CLOCK
CROSSTABLE
DEMO BOARD
DEMONSTRATION BOARD
FLAG
PAIRING CHARTS
PAIRING TABLES
RATING
SCORESHEET
SECOND
STAUNTON CHESS SET
THEORY
WALLBOARD
WHITE PIECES

J. MOVES RULES

■

ADJOURNMENT
AGREED DRAW
ARRAY
BISHOP
CAPTURE
CASTLE
CASTLE INTO CHECK
CASTLE KINGSIDE
CASTLE OUT OF CHECK
CASTLE QUEENSIDE
CASTLE THROUGH CHECK
CASTLING
CHECK
CHECKMATE
CHESSBOARD
DRAW
DRAW BY AGREEMENT
DRAW BY INSUFFICIENT MATING
  MATERIAL
DRAW BY PERPETUAL CHECK
DRAW BY REPETITION
DRAW BY STALEMATE
DRAW BY THE 50-MOVE RULE
DRAW BY THREEFOLD REPETITION
DRAWN GAME
EN PASSANT
FIDE LAWS OF CHESS
50-MOVE RULE
FORFEIT
ILLEGAL

ILLEGAL MOVE
ILLEGAL POSITION
INSUFFICIENT MATING MATERIAL
J'ADOUBE
KEEP SCORE
KING
KNIGHT
LAWS OF CHESS
LEGAL
LEGAL MOVE
LOSE
LOSE ON TIME
MATE
MOVE
MOVES AND RULES
PAWN
QUEEN
REPETITION OF POSITION RULE
RESIGNATION
RESIGNS
ROOK
RULES
SEALED MOVE
STALEMATE
THREEFOLD REPETITION
TIME CONTROL
TIME LIMIT
TOUCH-MOVE RULE
WIN

K. ENDINGS

■

BRIDGE
BUILDING A BRIDGE
COMPANION SQUARES
CONJUGATE SQUARES
COORDINATE SQUARES
CORRESPONDING SQUARES
CRITICAL OPPOSITION
CRITICAL SQUARE
CROSSOVER
DANCE OF DEATH
DIAGONAL MARCH
DIAGONAL OPPOSITION
DIRECT OPPOSITION
DISTANT DIAGONAL OPPOSITION
DISTANT OPPOSITION
HORIZONTAL OPPOSITION
KEY OPPOSITION
KEY SQUARE
KING MARCH
KNIGHT'S MOVE OPPOSITION
LONG-DISTANT DIAGONAL
  OPPOSITION
LONG-DISTANT HORIZONTAL
  OPPOSITION
LONG-DISTANT OPPOSITION
LONG-DISTANT VERTICAL OPPOSITION
MEANINGFUL OPPOSITION

OBLIQUE OPPOSITION
OPPOSITION
OPPOSITIONAL FIELD
OUTFLANKING
OUTSIDE CRITICAL SQUARE
OVERPASS
QUADRANGLE
QUADRANT
RECIPROCAL ZUGZWANG
RECTANGULAR OPPOSITION
RELATED SQUARE
RULE OF THE SQUARE
SISTER SQUARE
SQUARE OF THE PAWN
SQUEEZE
STAND IN OPPOSITION
TAKE THE OPPOSITION
THEORY OF CORRESPONDING
  SQUARES
THEORY OF CRITICAL SQUARES
TRÉBUCHET
TRIANGULATION
TURNING MANEUVER
UNDERPASS
UNIVERSE
ZUGZWANG

L. PAWNS

■

ADVANCED PAWN
BACKWARD PAWN
BALANCED PAWN STRUCTURE
BASE OF THE PAWN CHAIN
BAYONET ATTACK
BEHIND A PASSED PAWN
BIFFING THE BISHOP
BITING ON GRANITE
BLIND SIDE
BLOCKADE
BLOCKED
BLOCKED CENTER
BLOCKED PAWN
BREAK
BREAKTHROUGH
BREAKTHROUGH COMBINATION
CANDIDATE PASSED PAWN
CHAIN
CLASSICAL PAWN CENTER
CLOSE GAME
CLOSED CENTER
CLOSED FILE
CLOSED GAME
CLOSED OPENING
CLOSED POSITION
CONNECTED PASSED PAWNS
CONNECTED PAWNS
CRIPPLED MAJORITY
DOUBLED ISOLATED PAWNS
DOUBLED PAWNS
DYNAMIC CENTER
FIXED
FIXED CENTER
FIXED PAWNS
FLANK ATTACK
FREEING ADVANCE
FREEING MOVE
GAMBIT
HALF-OPEN FILE

HANGING PAWNS
HEAD PAWN
HOLE
ISLAND
ISOLANI
ISOLATED D-PAWN
ISOLATED PAWN
ISOLATED PAWN PAIR
ISOLATED QUEEN-PAWN
KICK
KING-PAWN GAME
KING-PAWN OPENING
LEVER
LITTLE CENTER
LIVE SIDE
LONG SIDE
LUFT
LUST TO EXPAND
MAJORITY
MAKE LUFT
MARÓCZY BIND
MINING OPERATION
MINORITY ATTACK
MOBILE CENTER
MOBILE PAWN CENTER
OPEN BOARD
OPEN CENTER
OPEN FILE
OPEN GAME
OPEN LINE
OPEN POSITION
OPENING A FILE
PASSED PAWN
PAWN CENTER
PAWN CHAIN
PAWN CONFIGURATION
PAWN DUO
PAWN ENDING
PAWN FORK

PAWN FORMATION
PAWN ISLAND
PAWN MAJORITY
PAWN PROMOTION
PAWN RACE
PAWN ROLLER
PAWN SKELETON
PAWN STORM
PAWN STRUCTURE
PAWN WEAKNESS
PERMANENT WEAKNESS
PHALANX
PROMOTION
PROTECTED PASSED PAWN
PUTTING THE QUESTION TO THE
  BISHOP
QUEEN-PAWN GAME
QUEEN-PAWN OPENING
QUEENING A PAWN
QUEENSIDE MAJORITY
QUEENSIDE PAWN MAJORITY
RELEASE OF TENSION
REMOTE CORNER
REMOTE FILE
REMOTE PASSED PAWN
SEMI-CLOSED
SEMI-CLOSED GAME
SEMI-CLOSED POSITION
SEMI-OPEN

SEMI-OPEN GAME
SEMI-OPEN POSITION
SHORT SIDE
SPLIT PAWNS
STEAMROLLER
STONEWALL
STONEWALL DEFENSE
STONEWALL FORMATION
STRONG POINT
STRONG-POINT DEFENSE
STRONG SQUARE
SUPPORT POINT
SUPPORTED PASSED PAWN
SYMMETRICAL PAWN STRUCTURE
TAKE TOWARD THE CENTER
TOWARD THE CENTER
TRIPLED PAWNS
UNBALANCED PAWN STRUCTURE
UNBLOCK
UNDERPROMOTION
UNDOUBLE
UNITED PASSED PAWNS
UNITED PAWNS
UNNECESSARY PAWN MOVES
WALL
WALLING IN
WEAK SQUARE
WEAKNESS
WIDENING THE FRONT

ABOUT THE AUTHOR

∎

Bruce Pandolfini is the author of sixteen instructional chess books, including *Chess Target Practice; More Chess Openings: Traps and Zaps 2; Beginning Chess; Pandolfini's Chess Complete; Chessercizes; More Chessercizes: Checkmate!; Principles of the New Chess; Pandolfini's Endgame Course; Russian Chess; The ABC's of Chess; Let's Play Chess; Kasparov's Winning Chess Tactics; One-Move Chess by the Champions; Chess Openings: Traps and Zaps; Square One;* and *Weapons of Chess.* He is also the editor of the distinguished anthologies *The Best of Chess Life & Review,* Volumes I and II, and has produced, with David MacEnulty, two instructional videotapes, *Understanding Chess* and *Opening Principles.*

Bruce was the chief commentator at the New York half of the 1990 Kasparov–Karpov World Chess Championship, and in 1990 was head coach of the United States Team in the World Youth Chess Championships in Wisconsin. Perhaps the most experienced chess teacher in North America, he is co-founder, with Faneuil Adams, of the Manhattan Chess Club School and is the director of the New York City Schools Program. Bruce's most famous student, six-time National Scholastic Champion Joshua Waitzkin, is the subject of Fred Waitzkin's acclaimed book *Searching for Bobby Fischer* and of the movie of the same name. Bruce Pandolfini lives in New York City.